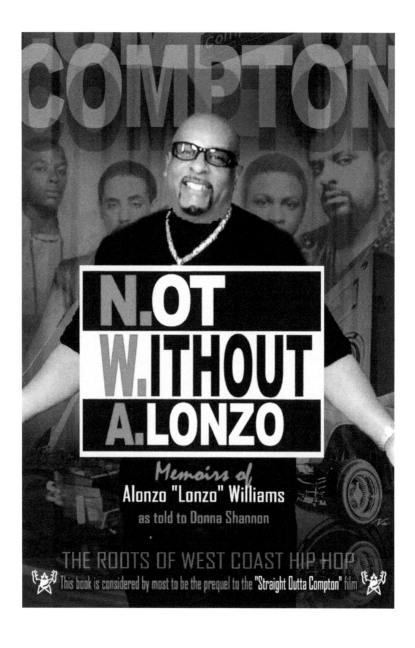

N.OT
W.ITHOUT
A.LONZO

Memoirs of
Alonzo "Lonzo" Williams
as told to Donna Shannon

ISBN-13: 978-0692536858 (The Lonzo Infotainment Co.)

ISBN-10: 069253685X

To

To my kids and grandkids, and the great grandkids that I may never meet, and to my family – both related and not related – because it's very important that we understand the legacy of the family in order to inspire the next generation to do bigger and better things. And to my dad and the generation that inspired and encouraged me to accomplish more than they did, and not to let money be my sole motivation for achievement.

Contents

Foreword
Acknowledgments
Introduction

Part I   Natural Born Hustler
Chapter 1   Family 1
Chapter 2   School 3
Chapter 3   Disco Lonzo, Roots of the Game 5

Part II   Opportunities Come Knocking
Chapter 4   Twist of Fate 15
Chapter 5   Doing Things My Way 25
Chapter 6   Alpine Village 29
Chapter 7   Lonzo Don't Play That 49
Chapter 8   Eve After Dark 62
Chapter 9   Young Baller 71
Chapter 10   East Rocks West........................... 76
Chapter 11   History of the Wrecking Crew 79

Part III   The Wreckin' Cru Introductions
Chapter 12   Dr. Dre 81
Chapter 13   DJ Yella 89
Chapter 14   Cli-N-Tel 92
Chapter 15   Shakespeare 94
Chapter 16   The Jackets 98
Chapter 17   Early Days 101
Chapter 18   Straight *Into* Compton!! 109
Chapter 19   Killing the Game – KDAY 114
Chapter 20   Launching the Wreckin' Cru 117

Part IV   The Record Biz Back in the Day

Chapter 21   The Feud that Fueled the West.......... 119

Chapter 22   Macola Records and Don MacMillan ... 125

Chapter 23   New York Partners 131

Chapter 24   The Macola Implosion 136

Chapter 25   What I Had to Deal With 139

Chapter 26   The Cru turning Off the Lights 147

Chapter 27   Big Hit, No Band 152

Chapter 28   Michel'le 156

Chapter 29   Back on the Road with a New Cru 162

Chapter 30   West Coast Record Distributors 170

Chapter 31   Pioneer in the Old West 180

Part V   N.W.A.

Chapter 32   Pre-NWA: Jerry Heller and Our
              Major Record Deal 187

Chapter 33   Reckless to Ruthless 201

Chapter 34   "Fuck the Police," Again - *What I Remember* 206

Chapter 35   Eric "Eazy E" Wright 210

Chapter 36   O'Shea "Ice Cube Jackson 218

Chapter 37   Kim "Arabian Prince" Nazel 222

Chapter 38   Lorenzo "MC Ren" Patterson 224

Chapter 39   Ultimatum 225

Part VI   Team Wreckin' Cru

Chapter 40   Shirley 229

Chapter 41   Swamp Dog 243

Chapter 42   Real Eyes Realize Real Lies 253

Chapter 43   America Loves a Gangster 261

Part VII   Responsibility

Chapter 44   To Whom Much is Given 268

Chapter 45   Summing It Up 271

Foreword

The terms "legend" and "legendary" are so loosely thrown around today. I hear people calling someone "legend" simply for the fact that they may have been around for years...but if you question them as to why that person is a legend, it's hard for them to explain.

You also hear stories about so-called "legends" who have made people think they are legends for their created "history" which often goes unchallenged because people enjoy the story more than the facts. It's very easy to get caught up in the myth. I've always laughingly told people that I don't want to be a legend, for most of the legends I know have passed on.

My description of a legend is someone who was a transformational figure in a particular field; someone who not only achieved success (and that's not always monetarily), but changed history and set a new direction in motion. A legend is someone who is able to create a new genre. Someone who "changed the course..." That describes Alonzo Williams, known to me and many others simply as "Lonzo."

I arrived in Los Angeles in July of 1983 to create the first ever "legendary radio station known for rap music" (although it would be characterized today as the first "Contemporary Hit Radio" (CHR) Rhythmic Radio Station, 1580 KDAY. It was because of Lonzo that I was able to begin my own legacy.

Creating the very first ever "Traffic Jam" in Radio— basically mixes that were played during afternoon drive traffic—I asked Lonzo if he knew of any DJs that were hot. Without hesitancy, he offered me the use of his DJs, Dr. Dre and DJ Yella. I had no clue what the future would bring for the history-making talent I now had DJing for me. People constantly ask me if we knew we were making history. NO! We were just having fun! I think if we had known we were making history, it wouldn't have been as much fun. There was no pressure back then, as there was no competition.

Not only did Lonzo offer their DJ services to me, but Lonzo helped ME get to know the streets of L.A., the dos' and don'ts of the streets, what colors not to wear, what hoods to be aware of…just an overall knowledge of the streets. Lonzo also taught me how to promote in the streets of L.A. Any promoter will tell you, each city is different to promote in; you have to change it up. In L.A., each *neighborhood* is different to promote in; Lonzo taught me that. It all began with Live Broadcasts from Dooto's Nightclub in Compton, and next door at Skateland U.S.A. for bigger parties.

In getting to know Lonzo, our friendship grew and still is strong today. You cannot be around him for more than five minutes without him saying something that will have you falling on the floor laughing, and he doesn't even recognize his sense of humor—that's just Lonzo!

The late Uncle Jamm's Army's Rodger Clayton and Lonzo were the party promoters for that generation of black youth when I arrived in L.A. I watched with huge admiration for how Lonzo took some kids (we called them kids, although they weren't much younger than we were) who had no knowledge of the business—period—and taught them enough that ultimately branched out to become Superstars on their own right, leading to what we now know as the

Biggest Grossing Music Biopic in the History of Movies…"Straight Outta Compton"!

Lonzo is where that all began…

One must understand how difficult it was for Lonzo to take these kids, run a tight ship, and in many ways, be a father type figure. He had to make hard decisions that were unpopular sometimes, but he pushed them, he guided them, he saw things they weren't able to envision. We're talking Dr. Dre, DJ Yella, and the lesser-known (but just as talented in their own respects) DJ Cli-N-Tel and Shakespeare—collectively first known to the world as the "World Class Wreckin' Cru."

When you take a look behind the scenes of any major superstar, there's a story…sometimes it's told correctly, sometimes it's not. It's much easier in today's fast internet world to know who's behind who, but back then you were left to hear stories, mostly inaccurate and mostly told by someone people admired at the time and so they were assumed to be telling the truth.

This is why I'm so excited that Lonzo is finally setting the record straight with this book, FINALLY letting you know with his own words where all the magic originated. I assure you, it will change what you've heard!

Greg "Mack Attack" Mack
West Coast Hip Hop Pioneer,
Formerly of 1580 KDAY

Acknowledgements

My dad, Alonzo Williams (R.I.P.), for encouraging and supporting me.

Jefty "Boss" Harris for giving me an opportunity to own my own club at the age of 22, and for all the wisdom he blessed me with.

Jai Rich (R.I.P.) for teaching me how to DJ and speak clearly.

Dr. David Horne for staying on my ass all these years.

Michael Concepcion for also keeping that bug in my ear.

Dr. Owen Robinson for keeping me healthy.

My attorney, Joseph Richardson, for keeping me out of court.

Steve Harvey for his book "Act Like a Success, Think Like a Success"—it helped me to get off my ass and make this book happen.

Nathaniel (Pops/Rolo) Taylor for always being there with a positive word.

My cousin Joel (Joe) Muwwakil (R.I.P.) for all the good times we had.

My brother, Randy (Suga Bear) Williams (R.I.P.), for having my back and helping me kick all that in the early days.

Jeannie "The Fairy Godmother" Billiteri; without her, I couldn't have done it.

Jerry "Swamp Dog" Williams for all the guidance, then and now.

Lonnie Simmons, a man I never met but who still influenced me.

Larkin Arnold, a major influence on my life.

Jheryl Busby (R.I.P.) for sending Cameo to my club, and for business advice.

Lewis Harper for bringing me into the record game.

Rodger (Mr. Prinze) Clayton (R.I.P.) from Uncle Jamm's Army for the feud that fueled the west.

Andre (Unknown DJ) Manuel for playing such big role in the forming of the west coast music scene.

All my kids and grandkids for motivating me to make sure my legacy didn't get swept under the rug: Erika Riley, Joshua, Jordan, Kristen, and Alonzo 3rd. Jamari, Dylan, Jaylen and Sophia.

Peanut for making the phone calls and hooking me up.

My cousin Askia for his daily motivational speeches, and for his contributions to the book.

Anthony "AK" King for the homie love and respect, and for his contributions to the book.

Charles Martin and Shakespeare for taking time out to contribute their recollections to the book.

My nephew Shak for always being more than family—also a friend.

Pastor Joe Robinson at Resurrection Church for keeping it real all the time.

Kingsley Jones for always being a voice of reason.

Dennene "Spiffy" Jones, aka superwoman.

Jarrette Fellows, my Editor-in-Chief.

To all the folks that rolled with me over the years—my crews from all my clubs, all the various members of World Class Wreckin' Cru, the Uzi Bros, Mona Lisa, Battle Cat, Richie Rich, Phaat Raat, Alberto, Willie Z, and George Claiborne.

My original crew—Billy Tee, Sweet Ron Ron, Dr. Rock and The Unknown DJ.

My recording crew—Mona Lisa, Cli-N-Tel, Dr. Dre, Yella, and Shakespeare, Michel'le, Big Curt, Frank, Will Rock, Banks, Ron Gray and Ken.

The brothers that always had my back—Whoop, Wendell, Vince, Charles, Eric (R.I.P.), Charles, Roscoe, Fat Fat, Big Chuck, Chilli Pete, Phantom, Sheri, Marsha, Velvet, Dana, and the EAD ladies and guys that supported us in our early days.

My cousin Veneta—a true ride or die "and she don't know what it means," and her daughters Talise and Lena.

Natosha, Donna, Sammy, Kenny, Iesha, La Shelle, Jerry, and Etta.

My record folks—Jim Callon JDC, Cletus, Kelvin, and Helen Anderson.

Huffy Hooks, Jr. (R.I.P.) for showing us all how to hustle records.

Steve (R.I.P.) and Sue Yano for all the sales and exposure at the Rodium Swap meet.

Bill Walker of Thump Records; Doug Young for getting it all popping.

Greg Mack for air play that help build all our careers.

Matthew McDaniels, the video historian.

Reggie Andrews for your support and advice.

DJ Thump for keeping my name ringing in Vegas.

Sandra Jones, my former attorney and still friend, and the Jones family, especially Rod ("RJ," R.I.P.).

Silky D, Bryan Franklin, Rene Smith, Edwin Vaultz, Greg of Ultra Wave for always hooking me up.

Dora Johnson for making me a scholar.

The folks from back in the day—Violet Brown, Rose, Dee, Def Jef, Warren G, Lil E, Mc Eiht, Slip, Mike T, Rocking Tom, Chuck Small, The Twins, Ric Rock, Jolly Joe, Eazy, Chill, Vick, Rudy, Snake, JJ Fad, Arabian Prince, Kevin Nash, Kevin Fleming, Rodney O, Joe Cooley, Laylaw,

Eygpt, DJ Flash, Crazy Dee, Jazzy Dee, Violet Brown, Teresa Randall-Price, Foote (R.I.P.), Booker (R.I.P.), George, Big Curt, Willie Moe aka N Deed, Victor Brooks, Patrick, D Vince, Matthew Brooks, Fred Shaw, Taboo, Lynette, Ms. Pam, Kinney, Whoop, Big O, Natosha, Meatball, Car Wash, LaShelle, Javoy, Big Ron, Jerry Doby, Sherry, Iesha and the dancers and customers of the Loft and Boom Boom Room, Darcell, Norris and Steve.

All my Facebook, Twitter and Instagram friends.

My Steppin' Family—Karen, Davita, Jeannie, Steve, Brian, Big Mike, Paula, Pam, Denise, Gary, Jackie…too many names to mention, but these are some of my main characters. To everyone on the dance floor around the country, much love.

To my family—April, Cynthia, Harold, Ryan, Lynn, Messy, Andrew, Eli, Alonnie, Aliya, Josie, Chis, Kent, Charles, Rene, Felice, Reggi, Renard, Izahia, Alonzo, Kim, Rodney, Azania, Azali, Jahad, Yamiya, Felicia, Najee, Jamal, Stephanie, Shonte, Eden, Zaire, Josh, Yolanda, Marsha, Phillip, Martha, Kim, Nicole, Big Chillz, Jonathan, June, and Ed.

Last but not least, Team Lonzo: Donna Shannon, writer/editor; Nik Quinn, graphics; Ed Sims, publicity; Shamika Brown, social media and marketing; Toni Odom, social media consultant; Rene Smith, personal assistant; Donn G. Shannon and E.B. Bluett, proofreaders.

I know with all the folks I have mentioned,
I am still gonna forget someone.
Please, for me it's not intentional.

Introduction

Hip-hop. Rap. The terms today conjure up visions of saggin', cussin', fuckin', murder, mayhem and doin' time. This is not the hip hop/rap I helped start on the west coast. They call me "The Godfather of West Coast Rap," and I humbly accept the title—well okay, maybe not so humbly, because it *is* the truth. I helped some of the biggest names in the game get started.

I am best known as "Lonzo," known worldwide as the World Class Grandmaster Leader of the **World Class Wreckin' Cru**. I discovered Dr. Dre, Ice Cube, and I played a major part in Eazy E's early career. I became a very instrumental source when it came to the Compton music and entertainment scene.

Hip hop was born on the east coast, spread to the west coast, and we took it in our own direction. When I started in the music business, it was all about having fun, making money, and getting babes.

My group, the World Class Wreckin' Cru, did R&B-ish hip hop. We were known best for our ballads. We had a hell of a ride until outside forces intervened with mis-information that caused dissension among us.

I watched west coast hip hop morph into something I no longer recognized. I'm not trying to discredit anyone, but in hip hop, "keepin' it *real*" is supposed to be what separates hip hop from other music genres. Unfortunately, hip hop has sold some of the biggest lies in history. Because of some of the images projected by hip hop artists over the years, impressionable individuals find themselves desensitized to life-altering situations from DUI's to life in the penitentiary. Young people are so influenced by all these lyrics. Rap artists don't realize the weight of the damage they leave behind while they're busy getting paid.

I've been blessed—I ain't been to the Pen, and I ain't trying to go. **Fuck** going! But I've seen enough cats get caught up trying to live up to the lyrics that somebody else wrote. Part of my motivation to write this book is that people need to know the *positive* roots of west coast hip hop. I was there in the very beginning. I *lived* this shit and I tell it just like it was—the way west coast hip hop really got started.

In the beginning, rap was only one of the many types of hip hop. But once the gangsta rap ship was launched from the City of Compton, it took over the world. Now we're beginning to see more of the biggest rap stars reaching back to assist the communities that helped to propel them into massive stardom and wealth. It's good to see.

Another reason I'm writing this book is that I'm tired of other people telling *my* story and getting it *wrong*. Those who know will love me for what I'm doing. Those who don't know will call me a hater and I'll be ridiculed—*fuck 'em!* I'll take that, because this story needs to be told. I'm hoping to prevent somebody else from falling into the trap that's being perpetrated by the desensitizing of young people to so many things that when I grew up *just did not fly!* I want to open young minds to the real history of hip hop, so maybe new artists will take an interest in taking the art back to the truth.

This book is the short version of forty years of entertainment experience, during which time I watched and experienced first-hand the evolution of the mindset and attitude of the community affected by rap music over the years. I had a direct behind-the-scenes, up-close-and-personal look into the creation, development, and effects of west coast rap.

I know this book will piss off people who don't want to believe there is no Santa Claus. A young kid who finds out there's no Santa Claus will sometimes get mad at the person who tells him the truth, as opposed to the person who lied and told him there is a Santa Claus in the first place.

If you still wanna believe in Santa Claus, this book might not be for you. But if you want to peek behind the curtain and see that the Wizard of Oz, Santa Claus, the Easter Bunny, and a lot of the biggest rap artists were all created with the same smoke and mirrors, then this book will open your eyes and mind to the power of music.

The members of N.W.A. ultimately moved on to bigger and better things, but they never abandoned their rap roots and now they've made a movie, Straight Outta Compton, chronicling their rise to the top of their game. I'm glad I waited to release this book until after I saw the movie. For entertainment value, I would give this movie a 10; the writing and acting were excellent. For historical accuracy, I'd have to give it a 5, understanding that the complexity of the story through all the years involved could not possibly be adequately told in one two-and-a-half hour movie, so some creative license had to be applied. Still, you get a good idea of what was going on during N.W.A.'s time. My character in Straight Outta Compton was a very outspoken individual—a lot like me in real life. I really was (and still am) a very outspoken person.

This book is considered by many to be the prequel to the movie, because it gives a lot of the history leading up to the formation and ascension of N.W.A.—a lot of details the movie didn't have time to include. In this book, you'll also see that I'm speaking my mind about a lot of things that I've been silent on for many years. Some folks will see a side of me they've never seen before, and some will be able to reaffirm their suspicions about me. Nonetheless, this is me. One thing I do very well is be myself.

I came into this world June 16, 1957, born and raised in Compton, California. I started in the music industry as a kid in my early 20's. Now, in the prime of my middle age, I look back and wonder, is there hope for the redemption of hip hop?

Sometimes in life, how significant a person is believed to be to a situation depends on who's got the money to tell the story. Well I got a few dollars, and I'm telling my story.

Lonzo
lonzo@lonzowilliams.com

"This guy was seriously the Berry Gordy of our time, if you really think about it and put it in context. The Eazy's, the Dre's, the Yella's—any of 'em—without Lonzo, who were they gonna go to? They did not know the industry...you had to have a "father figure" or a mentor to put you in the right vehicle. Without Lonzo, there was none of them..."

Charles Martin

Part I

Natural Born Hustler

*"Every man has to have
a good job **and** a good hustle."*
— *Dad*

1

Family

My dad, Al Williams, always told me to be an owner and not a renter. Dad taught me to do what you love and you'll never work hard a day in your life. He also taught me that every man has to have a good job *and* a good hustle. The job takes care of your family, and your hustle takes care of whatever else you like. I learned to hustle working with my dad.

My mom, Artomese Williams, didn't take no shit from nobody. If she thought that something was going down, she'd confront it. This was her natural personality. My mother was a natural fighter. She stood up for whatever she believed in. And a lot of times my dad would be behind her, "Oh, shit...okay..."

I had a brother, Randy, and two sisters, Cynthia and Martha. Martha was 11 years older than me. She was popular, and mom watched her like a hawk. We went to St. Albert the Great Catholic School in Compton. My parents weren't Catholic. They just wanted us to get a good education.

As a middle-age adult, I consider myself a spiritual person, but I'm sure as hell not religious. I've been Catholic, I've been Muslim…every time my girlfriend changes, my religion changes. I go with what works for me. But I go to church every week!

I might not consider myself a conventional Christian, but I'm a God-fearing man. I have my issues with Christian denominations, Islam—all of it. But I have enough sense to believe there is something bigger than me. And whether you call him Allah, Jesus, whatever the case may be—titles don't really mean anything. To me, it's the existence of the Being.

2

School

I'm a child of the 60's and 70's when corporal punishment was not even questioned. If you went to school, you got your ass whipped. There was no issue about that. No parents went up to the school to ask questions. That was part of your curriculum. You got Math, Science, English, and Ass-Whipping 101.

I went to St. Albert the Great Catholic School until seventh grade. After that, it was Vanguard Junior High in the Compton Unified School District. After Vanguard, I went to Centennial High. While at Centennial, some of my buddies and I tried our hand at some illegal activities. We got caught, but got away, and I learned a quick lesson about what I *didn't* want to do!

I left Centennial a couple months before 11th grade ended. I eventually was transferred over to Gardena High School, which at the time was only maybe twenty-five percent Black, and since I was from Centennial High School (which was considered at that time a rough high school), I had no problems at Gardena High just on pre-assumption! I was from a territory that was known for gang banging, so nobody messed with me. I graduated from Gardena High.

3

Disco Lonzo,
Roots of the Game

I've always been an innovator, even as a kid. My dad raised me like that. He taught me not to be afraid to be different. He used to say, "Don't be a follower, be a trend setter." And I was. If everybody else was doing one thing, I'd go do something else.

I always got clowned in school for being different. In the 70's when everybody else wore black leather jackets and black hats, I bought me a white leather jacket and a white beanie, and that's what I wore. That was my anti-gang statement.

One time a cop pulled me over…

"What are you wearing…what gang do you belong to?"

"Man, I'm just a good guy. I don't want y'all to get me confused."

The cop started laughing.

"Man, what kind of shit is that?"

"Hey man, my dad told me, why do I wanna be like everybody else?"

When I started doing music, when I started doing nightclubs, everybody else was running around the city trying to book a room. I was the first one to have his own nightclub on a regular basis. I didn't have to worry about trying to find a ballroom or a banquet hall. I had my *own* room. All those things I learned as a kid eventually helped me develop into who I am today.

My original name for DJ'ing was Disco Lonzo. When I started pursuing my DJ career, I didn't have any records. I never was a record collector, and I was always borrowing my buddy Wayne's records. Along with being work mates at Kinney Shoes in Compton, Wayne Ware and I were also the president and vice-president of the Charismatic Vega Club. Wayne had an extensive record collection. He also had a real nice house with a stereo system, and there was a component set and I would use that a lot to do my dances.

Wayne's girlfriend, Arlene, went to Regina Caeli High School, which was an all girls' school directly across the street from St. Albert's, my old elementary school. They needed a DJ for their dances, so I started booking those gigs, earning sixty bucks a night with the equipment provided, and I was *good*. Of all the DJs they ever hired, I was the only one they kept bringing back repeatedly. I'd give Wayne maybe $10 for using his records and stereo. I felt good. I was making money. I would DJ for that school every other week.

Regina Caeli dances were like vindication for being bullied at St. Albert's. This was a great gig for an upcoming DJ because, number one, *it's an all girls' school*. And most the girls were pretty—I'd have played for free just to be around all those girls. But the nuns at Regina Caeli were no joke! You couldn't play slow records. You played a slow record, they'd roll like I was still in school! They were something else.

Point of fact, they did the dances with no security at that time. This was in Compton, and the only security guards they had were Catholic nuns! The dances would go from 8 to 11. I only saw a security guard maybe once or twice later on in my reign at Regina Caeli, but on a normal night, there would only be nuns and a few parents handling security. And we're talking about a *flood* of kids—200 kids at a school with me DJ'ing. Maybe a few dads, but no armed guards, no cops—and nothing happened!

While I was DJ'ing at Regina Caeli, some of the nuns who worked at St. Albert's had been transferred to Regina Caeli. They knew me from going to St. Albert's. The nuns were the chaperones/security guards at this time for these dances. And like I said, they didn't allow me to play slow records. But the girls loved me to play slow records! They kept asking for slow records. Every time I played one, the nun would come over and warn me, "We don't play those here."

The warnings got more serious. Finally the nun told me, "If you play another slow record, you will never play here again." I played another one. The nun took a ruler, knocked the needle off the record, grabbed me by my ear (I'm 19 years old!), put that ruler to my nose like it was a pistol and said, *"Do it again and see what happens!!!"* Needless to say, those girls never got any more slow records.

This is how far back I go to the scene of entertainment in Compton. I've seen guys get jumped at dances. It would be a jealousy thing for the most part, but back then nobody ever really got hurt. Nobody ever got stomped out where they had to be carried home or put in an ambulance. Guys would have their little squabbles and then it would be over.

During the Regina Caeli days, I drove a '73 Chevy Vega that looked like a mini-Camaro. It allowed me to join a car club, the Charismatic Vegas. We would give dances to generate money. Wayne Ware was the president of the car club; I was the vice president. We gave our first dance at the Chester Washington Golf Course. We grossed about $1500 that night! We only had to spend maybe $600 to pay for everything we needed. We were doing the dance to buy jackets for our members. The jackets were maybe $3 or $4 a piece. Everything included—dance, money, everything—I think we spent about $600 and we made about $900 profit.

Fortunately for me and Wayne, we were the only ones that invested any money, so we had change left over, and we split the money up. And that's when I realized I wanted to be a promoter *and* a DJ. Understand the time...we're talking about the mid-70's when disco records are being played, a lot of R&B, and we're right there in the middle.

I've personally experienced numerous musical genres, from a kid growing up in heavy blues, R&B, and black revolutionary R&B; then the disco era hit, then the funk era hit; then hip hop and rap came along. At this time, we're on the cusp between R&B and disco. I wanted to be part of that. I just didn't know how to do it at first, but my reputation as a DJ started to grow because I always put on a show. I wore a construction hat with a light on top of it. I had a custom-made tee-shirt with a superman emblem on it that said "Disco Lonzo, Superstar DJ," along with whistles and various sound effects. I was always taught to fake it 'til you make it.

I wore this tee-shirt and hat everywhere I DJ'd. By this time, because the disco era was taking off so well for the White people and the middle-upper class, young Black promoters started doing events in hotels and we billed them as disco dances. There were no Black disco clubs back then. Most of the clubs were for 21 and over. We had a couple of clubs that let you in at 18, but they were always in the white area and they always gave us a hassle.

Dance Parties and Clubs

My old man saw me making money, so he loaned me some money to purchase two Sanyo turntables. Believe it or not,

I still have one of them forty years later and it still works! This would be the beginning of my mobile DJ career.

After purchasing speakers, I used the skills I learned in shop classes back in junior high and from helping my dad around the house to build my own stand with my name on it, "Disco Lonzo," in big red letters.

I was becoming a favorite among the DJ request list, meaning I was always getting requests to do parties.

Dance parties were one of the hustles we had back in the day. As a DJ, it was hard for me to get gigs in the beginning because of my lisp, but I was persistent. I'm a natural-born hustler—that's what I do. My dad gave me that trait. I was determined that I would not be denied, and I eventually became one of the more popular DJs.

Charles Martin remembers…

"We were not that far under Lonzo age-wise, but we were out doing parties at people's homes, receiving cash, and in a Rolling 60's neighborhood when gang-banging was full-fledged. Wasn't like, "Time out, nigga, you get a pass.' It was like, 'Where you from?' For real! You're talkin' 'bout the '70's, early '80's.

"Right now, you'd probably get a pass, but back then, it was like they were tryin' to prove something more than anything, and you had to be careful of what music you played! You're at somebody's house, you gotta play what they like. You still gotta take your shit out of their house!

"I started off with Lonzo back in '76, '77. We were doing from house parties to Tahitian Village, Alpine Village—you name it. Then he started dealin' with Uncle Jam's Army, LSD Promotions, and so on. Overall, I still think Lonzo's the Berry Gordy of South Central, and I mean that wholeheartedly. He's been a great mentor of mine.

"We're talkin' over 37 years ago. When it's all said and done, the good, the bad, the ugly—good dude. I learned so much about entrepreneurism from watching him. That's one of the biggest reasons for me being an entrepreneur today. I love this dude, no BS, this is straight from the heart. He was and is like a father figure to me.

"Overall, when you get Dre who came in after me, Eazy E—I really didn't know them 'cause I had kinda left the organization before they came in. I think when I left, Dre had just started; he took over my spot. I used to be a DJ—and I know I couldn't DJ for shit! Lonzo used to fuss...

'Get his ass off that damn thing!'

"I can hear him now. 'Cause I would play the same songs over and over—it sounded good to me, hell!"

I was one of the only DJs at that time that had any kind of broadcast experience, so I got hired for a lot of gigs. Some promoters had their own in-house DJs and I would fill in for them from time to time. I was always on the scene. Whether I was providing the sound, doing pre-promotional entertainment, doing an after-party or a picnic, I was always providing entertainment. A lot of times I would go to a dance as a spectator. Maybe the DJ they hired had a little bit more notoriety but he couldn't handle the crowd, so they would grab me at the front door…

"Hey, Lonzo's here, man!"

They would grab me by the arm, put me on the turntables, and I'd turn the whole party around.

Understanding Music and People

I didn't just lay back and play records; I set you up for an event. Records are played to stimulate emotion; it's not just a flat record-playing situation. You play with a reason; you play for a purpose. Like playing chess—you play one record with another record in mind already, so you know where you're going before you get there.

I had learned how to program in broadcast school, which is something that most guys even today don't know how to do. And my reputation was pretty big! I had this sign that said, "Disco Lonzo," I had this hat, I had my business cards… I considered myself as being a professional long before being a professional was even cool.

Part II

Opportunities Come Knocking

"You don't have to be great to get started, but you have start to be great."
— *Les Brown*

4

Twist of Fate

In 1975, when I got ready to graduate from Gardena High School, I received a scholarship to go to broadcast school through the Regional Occupational Program. I graduated from Gardena High, turned eighteen years old, and had a daughter all within a seven-day period. My mind was going crazy, but I was on my way to broadcast school.

The school was called the Don Tracy School of Broadcasting. It was on Marlton and Santa Barbara (now Martin Luther King Boulevard). It's no longer there. It was a six-month course and I learned how to be a radio broadcaster from Don Tracy and Jai Rich. They taught us mixing (no beat mixing, just straight fading) and tape splicing. We also learned how to write and produce commercials. The only goal was not to have dead air. I learned how to do this, and this would later be incorporated into my mobile DJ skills.

I graduated from Tracy with a third class broadcast license, and the opportunity to go to work in Mississippi and a couple of other secondary markets. Unfortunately, at that time my mom was diagnosed with ovarian cancer and I was kind of designated by the family to transport her back and forth to chemo.

Knowing that she was in Stage 4 and was going to pass in a very short amount of time, I didn't take the job. Being only 19 years old at the time, I just wasn't really thinking about going to Mississippi anyway. This was a rough time in my life.

Caltrans Summer Job

After I did the summer Regional Occupational Program in the broadcast school, there was a program called CETA (Comprehensive Employment and Training Act). During the summertime, kids from the ages of fifteen to maybe eighteen could get jobs working for the County—Parks & Recreation, or whatever the case may be—to keep them out of trouble.

I retired from DJ'ing back in the 70's during a period when I was working for Caltrans during the summer. My daughter and her mom (Diane, my high school sweetheart) came to live with me.

With a newborn daughter, my old man was sweating me to get a good job. He had plans for me to have a secure long-term job following in his footsteps at Caltrans. He gave me the old "son, be a man" speech:

> "You got benefits. You got to be a fool to get fired from Caltrans you'd have to take stupid classes to get fired from Caltrans. You can make yourself some money and DJ on the weekend.
>
> "All this DJ'ing and running up and down the streets being out all time of night…you got a daughter now. You need to start thinkin' like a man, not a kid. You got a good girl over here, you got a house…you need to go on and be a family."

My dad always looked at my DJ'ing as just a hustle, like his gardening service was for him. For a *real* job, he expected me to follow in his footsteps at Caltrans.

At that time in my life, I was not interested in being a traditional family man. It never was my desire to get married and have a bunch of kids and go on vacation. I love all my kids and I spend time with all my kids, but I do it in a different way.

When I roll with my kids, it's just me and my kids! But because my dad had so much influence on me, I tried it. I gave up my turntables. I was working full time at Caltrans, but only during the summertime. I was turning down gigs because I had to work on Saturday.

Record Shack

Record Shack was a local record distributor in Compton on Walnut St. that sold mostly disco and rock music. I got offered a job there when I was trying to buy records wholesale. They offered me a job in Sales; I passed it to my buddy Rodger and he took the job.

After a while, Rodger told me about an opening in the warehouse. So I started off working in the warehouse pulling orders to be shipped to stores around the country. It was a part-time job that I worked in the evenings after I got off from Kinney's shoes (also in Compton).

It Almost Didn't Happen

Time passed and I took the test for Caltrans. I passed the test with flying colors because I'd been prepped all my life for it. I'm mechanically inclined, my dad had me working in the lawnmower shop, and I had worked in my dad's gardening service on weekends before I started DJ'ing. I knew all my tools and how to do different things, plus because I'm ROTC, I had leadership skills. I knew how to think. I scored like in the top two percent on the Caltrans test or something crazy like that. When I turned twenty-one, it wasn't long before Caltrans called me.

Trying to do the sensible thing and follow my dad's plan for my life, I put in my two week notice in at the Record

Shack. At Cal Trans, my dad was in landscaping. He trained me in landscaping, but I liked maintenance crew better. It was dirty, but I trained with a maintenance crew and I had buddies in maintenance. I was really thinking about going into maintenance.

Dead Crew on My Mind

There was a big cloud hanging over my head, though. One by one, almost my entire crew had gotten killed on the freeway— guys I hung out with every day rolling up and down the freeway. The first incident when two or three of them got killed was in what's known as a sweeper train. They were on the freeway one night with a big truck with a big impact box on the back of it so in case of impact, it wouldn't tear the truck up. There was another truck to pick up something, a street sweeper in front of that, and another truck that picked up all the heavy stuff the street sweeper couldn't pick up.

On the transition from the 91 to the 710, a big rig lost control and killed two or three of my partners. It was a big rig diesel truck, so they didn't have a chance.

One of my main trainer/mentors (and a good friend of my dad's) would normally have been working with this crew, but he was off that night. So he didn't get killed that night, but after that, he decided to switch to the sign crew. He was putting a sign up on the 405 one day and got hit by a car. They dragged him from Wilmington all the way to about

Long Beach Blvd. His body parts were found all over the freeway.

All this is in the back of my mind the whole time I'm thinking about whether I really want to work for Caltrans. I was excited about it at first, but now there was only one other guy in my crew that hadn't been killed, so I really wasn't that enthused about the Caltrans thing anymore.

There was also another down side. I was trying to build my DJ business, and I had to be up at 5:30, 6:00 a.m. to go across town to work at Caltrans. Most of the time, by 7:00 I'm putting sprinklers on the freeway. When trucks pass by doing 55, the water from the sprinklers tends to soak you. You spend most of your day trying to dry off. Then when it's not cold, I'm on the crack-sealing crew, which meant I had to sit in a little basket and pour tar between the concrete and the asphalt of the freeway. The hardest part for me about that was staying awake. I couldn't drive the truck because I'd fall asleep. I hated being in the basket because I fell asleep, not to mention I had to put highway cones out while dodging cars—my head was always over the side of the truck putting out cones. It was one of the most dangerous jobs I ever had in all my life.

It seemed I was in for almost certain death working on the sweeper train, and the odds seemed almost as high that I'd get maimed sealing cracks from the basket. On top of that, working for Caltrans I was nowhere near a phone the whole time. There were no beepers or cell phones back then, so the only way I could get a gig was somebody would call the house and when I got home that evening, I'd call them back—if I had the energy. When I worked at Record Shack, I worked in an air-conditioned warehouse—on roller skates, high most of the time, pulling records off the shelves and taking them to the shipping department. I came to work clean every day.

Divine Intervention
Lessons and Blessings

So all this was in the back of my mind. But again, because my dad's influence on me was so powerful, I turned down the Record Shack job and was headed to work for Caltrans.

When I got to Caltrans, they had this big board, like a mailbox almost; it had all these different documents in it, and the guy would grab a document off each one of these shelves and I had to put in all this paperwork to go to work for Caltrans. Well, they gave me my helmet, my shirt, and I did all the paperwork. This was on a Friday morning. I was in the process of sealing the deal when Divine Intervention stepped in.

"Hey, little money maker, I'm sorry man, but we don't have no insurance papers. We gotta get a copy from the district office. You can start to work on Monday."

This was all I needed. This had to be a sign, an omen. I left there and told myself, *I ain't going back.* I knew that a "forever" job and traditional family—that was my dad's plan for me, but I had another plan altogether. But how do I **not** go back when my dad is probably gonna kill me when he finds out I don't wanna work for Caltrans? He had pumped it up like it was the Super Bowl.

I called Dale, my supervisor at Record Shack and asked him if the job was still available.

"Yeah…what you gonna do?"

"I'ma take it!"

I went by Record Shack and talked to Dale before I went home.

My dad talked about my future with Cal Trans all Friday evening, talked about it Saturday, and Sunday evening I told him.

"Hey man, I'm not taking the Caltrans job. I'm gonna stay with Record Shack."

I've always been my dad's favorite kid, it's no secret. But now, for the first time in my life, I was a dumb-assed son-of-a-bitch. He cussed me out!

"What the fuck are you doing? You got a good civil service job, you're gonna be there forever, you can retire in 20 years with benefits, blah blah blah…"

"That ain't what I want to do, dad."

He couldn't understand it. He knew almost everyone I had trained with had gotten killed on the job; he told me to go into landscaping. Most of the time, the landscape guys were off to the side off of the freeway. You very seldom heard about the landscape guys getting hit. You had to be a damn fool to get hit in landscaping.

Maintenance guys are the ones that actually close the traffic on the freeway when something goes wrong. They're the ones that tend to block the freeways when there's an accident and they gotta pick up car parts, and sometimes body parts.

At that time, my old man had been working in landscaping about twenty years. He didn't have any problem, so he figured I wouldn't have any problem either. But I didn't want any part of that. He had put it to me a long time ago, "Be your own man, think for yourself." But the first time I did it with him, he wasn't going for it. He didn't appreciate it.

"Oh my God, I done trained this dumb muthafucka all his life, he gets a job at Caltrans, and now he don't want to do it?"

Oh, we fell out—for the first time in my life, we fell out.

"Them white folks, they gonna use you! They'll keep you around for five or six months and then they gonna fire your ass! You're gonna be looking for a job, Caltrans ain't gonna be hiring, and you're gonna be stuck."

To go against my dad at twenty-one years old, to forego all the dreams and plans he had for me, to want to go into music—it was crushing for him. After he ranted and raved to the point where I thought he was going to have a stroke or a heart attack, with tears of frustration in his eyes, he calmed down.

"Fuck it, it's your life. You can fuck it up anyway you want to. But don't come crying to me when they fire your ass in six months."

I think my dad respected my hustle, but he didn't understand that in my mind that hustle *was* the job. Working at Record Shack allowed me to build my DJ'ing supply of records. Actually, rather than just a job, I was growing my own business. It took a while before he could see it that way.

5

Doing Things My Way

For the first time in my life, I was making a move without my dad's blessing. It was a hell of a turning point in my life. I still was daddy's boy at heart, but I had to be my own man, too. I took the job back at Record Shack while I continued to push hard at my DJ-ing.

I went back to Record Shack bright and early Monday morning, but when I got to Record Shack, shit wasn't right. Half the people that worked in the sales office on Friday were gone on Monday, including my buddy Rodger. I was scared to DEATH! I've never been so scared in all my life. Not only was Rodger gone, they put me at Rodger's desk and gave me Rodger's phone log and his accounts to call. I'm sitting at my (Rodger's) desk, and I am totally confused.

I couldn't figure out what in the hell happened. She's gone, he's gone—about five people who I know who are regular salespeople are *gone*. I'm sitting there along with a couple of other new people I had never seen before, and Dale, the general manager, walks in with Curt, the Sales manager, and talks to us.

"Hey—as you can see, we had some changes over the weekend. We hope that you guys can step into their shoes and do a better job."

Now I'm sitting there wondering what in the hell I had gotten myself into. The first phone call I got was Rodger Clayton.

"Who's this…Lonzo? What you doing at my desk, man?"

"Rodger I don't know what's going on!"

"Man, those white boys just prejudiced, they prejudiced. They put Black man against Black man. You working with the white boys against me, man. That's fucked up."

"Rodger, I don't know nothin' about this, man!"

"Yeah man, you probably against me too. I know it, I know it. That's okay, that's okay. I'ma show all ya'll."

"Rodger, I thought you was gonna be in here sittin' next to me, doc. I don't know what you talking about man!"

"Man, that's fucked up, that's fucked up, that's fucked up!"

And so I'm sitting there looking stupid, feeling worse, and just confused, nervous, scared—all of the above. I got my dad on my shoulder; I got my so-called friend pissed off at me. I don't know what I'm doing; I don't know how to make these phone calls. But I know how to use the phone, so I start calling people up. First thing they wanna know is, "Where's Rodger at?" I explain that Rodger's not with us anymore and I'm the new salesperson, my name's Lonzo, blah blah blah...

Everything was going cool for a while. Rodger would call every day, though. Although he kept telling me that I stole his job, we still stayed in contact. About two months later, I guess the company had second thoughts about it, and they brought Rodger back into the sales room.

Rodger was a *great* salesman. Rodger knew music, he knew record labels, he knew distribution companies—he knew everything. Rodger's problem was, if he made $10K by noon, he wasn't coming back to work after lunch. He was taking the rest of the day off. He figured he got his quota for the day. White folks figured if you sold $10K by noon, you could probably make another five by 2:00. Rodger's theory was, *fuck them!* He didn't care. He was good. He was also very cocky. He was good at what he did and he was arrogant.

When they brought Rodger back to the sales room, we picked up where we left off. On the way to work in the morning, we'd be smoking weed having a *good* time— Rodger, my brother, and me. Go into work high, 'cause we didn't have to do anything all day long but get on the phone.

My brother was a weed head, Rodger was a weed head, and I was a weed-head in training. That's what we did. And at lunch time, we'd go get baked again. It was the 70's, we could do that. Nobody was drug testing. I'm clean every day. I'm in air conditioning. I'm comfortable. If I had a line on a gig, I'd call the people up…as long as they saw you on the phone, Record Shack didn't really care. Plus, I was able to build up my record collection at the same time.

6

Alpine Village

As a DJ, I quickly advanced to making $150 bucks a night. Back then, that kind of money meant you were getting **paid**. That meant you had to bring out lights, sound system, everything, and you'd get $150 bucks.

I'm working a lot, but not making the caliber of money that I feel I should be making. I'd be hired by promoters who passed out flyers and hung up posters to promote. I figured hell, I can do everything that they're doing! I'm clearing $100-$125 a night while they are profiting $800.00 to $2,000 a night off of *my* skills.

I've always been one for self-pimping... *"If thou shall be pimped, let it be done by thyself."* After a while, because I got tired of feeling like I was being pimped, I kinda started competing with the promoters. I started promoting my parties and making my own money. I started partnering up with other promoters to keep my flow going. My company was called Disco Construction.

My very first partner was Rodger Clayton of Uncle Jamm's Army. I was known as Disco Lonzo and he was the Ace of Dreams. We played Alpine Village on a regular basis. The place would be packed with at least three to five hundred kids coming out to party. Most of the time I was just his DJ, but before long I would be doing Alpine Village myself.

My brother Randy assisted me. He was cheap labor. He loved playing records, too, and his size came in handy when I had to deal with non-paying promoters. He liked playing tough, so we had a ball.

Being a promoter back in the day was totally different from what we have today. Back in the day, as young promoters, we were a group of young hustlers. Young hustlers who didn't sell dope. We sold entertainment. We found a niche that nobody else had, and we jumped into it.

On the West Coast, there were no Black discos. Although disco music was on radio, television, and in the movies, it was not in the hood. So like always, we made a way. Young Black promoters began renting hotel ballrooms all over the city to throw "Disco Dances."

In the 70's and 80's, disco dances were the ultimate "clean" hustle. The media created the disco hype and we just filled the void. Although we played some disco records, most of music consisted of R&B.

We were doing dances at the Queen Mary, the Convention Center, Holiday Inn in Universal City, Ramada Inn, Biltmore Hotel—every hotel that had a ballroom, we would put some young Black folks in it with little to no problem. Most of the time we were welcome to return.

There were several Black promoters: LSD Promotions, Z Cars, Elite Promoters, Uncle Jamm's Army, and my company—Disco Construction—to name a few. We started doing our own parties in the Black community or in hotels, whatever the case may be. We specialized in providing entertainment for Black teens and young adults.

Disco Construction and the Wrecking Crew (this was before we found out we had to change the name) soon became one of the largest promotion crews in the city. We had folks partying with us from as far as Pomona and the Valley.

The Wrecking Crew was the classiest and coolest crew, with our envied trademark reversible satin jackets and Morris Day/Prince-type attire combined with our girls being fashioned after Vanity 6. We had some of the sexiest females around—it made us the *shit*.

There were multiple facets of the Wrecking Crew, although we were one unit. Some guys did promotions, some guys did cleanup, and some guys did DJ'ing, and some guys did all three. *Everybody* was supposed to be a part of the security force, but not everybody did their part.

Imposter at Work

I remember one night a friend of mine from LSD Promotions, Larry Grigsby, called me from the Consolidated Plaza.

"Man, there's a guy up here doin' your whole show!"

"What are you talkin' about?"

"Man, the guy got a hat, he got on a tee-shirt, and he's sayin' all your shit with all your lines right now!"

So I went up to the Consolidated Plaza, a venue up in L.A., and Rodger and Andre (Unknown DJ) were doing a dance there. There they were, doing a bootleg version of the Disco Lonzo show. I used to wear a construction hat with a light on top of it. Andre had on a top hat. I had a black tee-shirt that said "Disco Lonzo" with a Superman emblem in the middle of it saying "Superstar DJ." I don't know what his said, but the design was the same. He looked like me except for the hat. He was doing my whole routine!

Larry was still there. He was laughing because he was the one that called me. I didn't get mad. I didn't really trip. It seemed like they were trying to take advantage of the Disco Lonzo popularity and style, but that night it rained so hard that nobody showed up.

From that point on, that's when Andre and I kinda clicked. Andre started hanging out at my house. A few weeks went by and we started kicking it. I found out he was from Detroit. I'm three years older than he is, and I was about 21, so he must have been about 18.

Rodger didn't really click with the clique until about a few weeks later. He was around, but he really didn't click with me until after I got him a job at Record Shack. I didn't really get to know him until then.

One day while I was still working at Record Shack, Rodger gets this idea he's gonna start promoting parties at Alpine Village over in Torrance, and conveniently, I was the DJ resource. When he asked me to DJ for him at Alpine, I was ready.

The gigs were okay. No real big money—I was getting like $75 or $100 bucks a night. That was a nice increase from Regina Caeli, but it still was a little low. This also reignited the promotional seed that was planted with the Charismic Vegas.

My father was very instrumental in my career. In fact, he was my very first investor. He rented equipment for me, got a line of credit for me…he really played a major role in helping me get my DJ'ing career off the ground.

Unfortunately, he's no longer here with me, but I definitely showed my appreciation to him when he was here. That's something I'll never forget.

Me and My Dad

By this time, I'm renting a sound system from a place in Hawthorne called Hogan's House of Music. I was able to rent a small band PA system for $35.00 a night. I'm still profiting $65.00, so I'm still winning. I'm DJ'ing all over the city now, killing game. My hustle was paying off. In fact, I got so good that when I wasn't gigging, I would rent out the equipment to other DJs and sometimes, because Hogan's was closed on Sundays, I would rent the equipment out to fashion shows on Sunday. I finally made enough profit to purchase my own amplifier, and shortly after that, I purchased my own speakers. Now I'm keeping all of my earnings. Man, I was rolling, balling out of control.

My old man decided to help buy me a van. Now, I'm one of the most sought out DJs, but there was this other DJ who used a huge Cerwin Vega system—that system was like the Rolls Royce of systems. The mixer itself ran about $600.00. In my case, that might as well have cost a million. My First DJ system was a Newark—not New*mark*. Newark was an electronics company like Radio Shack. They had a credit system that let you apply to get a line of credit from them. My monthly payment to them was $15.00 a month.

It took me almost two years to pay them off for a mixer that cost $129.00. I had my turntables, tops, amps, and mixers. I was gigging all over L.A. There are not many hotels in Los Angeles that were built in the 70's and 80's that have not been filled with sounds of Disco Lonzo.

So I'm DJ'ing for Rodger's dances at Alpine Village. As Rodger started making a little bit more money, I asked him for a slight raise. Pay me $125 or something! He wouldn't do it. The dances started getting bigger and bigger, and I couldn't get $125? I'm like, "Man, I gotta rent more equipment and speakers. My system is not big enough for this right here." So he finally let me get $150.

Shortly after that, Alpine Village became the go-to place for promoters. I'm the DJ. I got this big sign again, "Disco Lonzo," and I got the tee-shirt, "Superstar DJ Disco Lonzo."

I began to realize that at $150 a night, if I worked Friday, Saturday, and sometimes Sunday doing a baby shower or wedding reception, I could make between three and five hundred dollars a weekend working three days a week. At Record Shack, I was working five days a week, only making $162 a week.

I ain't ever been a genius, but I could do the math. For a month or so working at Record Shack, I was working basically just to get paid in records, but that was cool because it let me build up my record collection.

At Alpine Village, I'd always be the DJ, although Rodger was also a DJ. I had the equipment, but it was his party for the most part. He would wait until I got the crowd pumped up and ready to crack, and he'd run up to the DJ podium…

"Alright, man—I got it, I got it, I got it."

He'd push me off the stage and take over. Then he would try to take credit for having the party jumping! We always fought about that.

Rodger's DJ name was the Ace of Dreams. I was Disco Lonzo. We both had costumes. Rodger had a genie outfit with a cape on it, and he bought this magic dust that he would put in his hand and he'd light it with incense and a big flame would come up. These were our antics as DJs!

One night a fight broke out at Alpine Village. This one guy went berserk. Just went through the crowd kicking ass for no reason. It was like watching a movie.

Rodger had just made it to the stage and he was DJ'ing. I'm on the side and I see this rolling crowd of problem working toward the stage. All of a sudden the record went off and we had no music, just dead air, and I'm like, *where the fuck is Rodger?*

Alpine Village had a patio outside with sliding glass windows at the time. I'm not lying, this is the honest-to-God truth—Rodger was outside on the patio in a karate stance. This guy had a bumper jack handle with so much blood on it, blood was running down his arm.

Rodger's standing here in a karate stance and his cape is flapping in the wind like Superman and shit. This guy is about to whip Rodger's ass with the bumper jack handle. I'm going, *oh shit, what are we gonna do?* Somehow, the guy never hit Rodger with the bumper jack handle.

Only a handful of guys remember this story. Rodger's partner from Uncle Jamm's Army, Gid Martin, remembers the story. He told this story on one of the radio interviews we had after Rodger died. It was typical Rodger. Rodger was a control freak—a very smart dude with a memory like an elephant. He would talk shit without thinking. He'd get himself into situations and sometimes he didn't have enough sense to back down. I never figured out whether that was stupidity or courage.

My Fairy Godmother

Along comes a lady who decided she wanted to rent Alpine Village and make some money for herself and her daughters. Gid referred her to me. Her name was Jeannie Billiteri. She called me on the phone at Record Shack.

"Got your number from Gid Martin. I'm throwing a dance Friday night at Alpine Village and I need a DJ. Are you available?"

"Yeah!"

I told her I would charge her $150.

"No problem. Also, I want some lights at my party; I don't want just a regular dark room."

"I don't mind bringing lights, but I gotta get some money up front for the lights."

"No problem. Where you at?"

I told her to come to the office and ask for me, because I could have people come to the office. People were always coming to the office to pick up records COD or whatever.

She walked into the receptionist's office and the guy who hired me, Alonzo, couldn't believe it.

"Are you sure you're dealing with Alonzo *Williams?*

"I'm looking for Alonzo Williams, the DJ."

So he called me.

"Lonzo!"

"Yeah, man?"

"Man, there is a beautiful woman in the hallway lookin' for you!"

I walked out to the reception area, opened the door, and standing there is this half Italian, half Black sister, built like all outdoors. I looked at her, she looked at me, and we both started grinning. I remember like yesterday—she had long black hair, and she was sexy to the third degree.

She was definitely my type of woman. I was only twenty-one years old, but I figured with enough lies and bullshit maybe I could handle it. She gave me the money without any problems, enclosed inside of an envelope. I thought that was very professional of her.

Jeannie Billiteri was a very important part of what I did in the very early stages of my career. I nicknamed her my "Fairy Godmother." As a grown man, I would introduce her to people as my "Fairy Godmother," only because of our business relationship. We never took it any further than that, despite the mutual attraction. It was always business. We would flirt back and forth, but it was just that—flirting.

41

Jeannie Billiteri

Every promoter in town was jealous of our relationship. When she walked into the room, heads turned and they all were like, *she's with Lonzo*. It just made me feel good to have a pretty woman around, but they didn't know the relationship was nowhere near what they would have liked for it to be. We weren't sleeping together. She liked me and I liked her. She was a little older; she might have been 35, but there was a definite attraction. She drove a Corvette. I loved that Corvette. I thought I had died and gone to heaven.

Rodger got mad at Gid for turning Jeannie on to me, and he got mad at Jeannie for booking Alpine Village, because in his mind it was like he *owned* Alpine Village and nobody else had the right to go there. He always thought he owned any venue that he rented. He forgot it was open to the public.

Rodger was also mad at me because I DJ'd for *him* at Alpine Village. In his mind, I shouldn't DJ there for *her*. He felt I was betraying him. I told Rodger he was out of his damn mind.

Anyway, when she gave me the money to go get the lights, it was like 2:30. I didn't get off work until 3:30. I'm in Compton; the lights are in Hollywood on Sunset and Vine at Olsen Lighting Company. I called and made the reservation. They told me to come at 4:30 on the dot.

Now this is a true story. I scooped up my cousin, Joel, and we had like thirty minutes to get from Compton to Hollywood in semi-rush hour traffic. It didn't look good for the home team at all, but I had to impress this lady. I was determined to get this lady some lights.

We drove down Crenshaw to Rossmore with our heads hanging out the window of my van making ambulance sounds, *howling*. I'm not lying—people were pulling over and we made it from Compton to Hollywood with five minutes to spare by imitating ambulances when we got stuck in traffic.

This is the honest to God truth. People think I'm lying, but no. I used to do it real well, imitating that siren sound. I can't do it anymore. And my cousin would be imitating the horn (boo-doom, boo-doom, boo-doom), and people would pull over and let us go by.

We got to Olsen just as they were about to close the gate. The guys recognized me and let me in, they didn't pull the gate down to the shipping room, and we got what we needed.

Well, her gig did not do well at all. Alpine Village at the time held about eight hundred people; she had about forty. Even with the lack of success, she still had the money to pay me and to pay Alpine.

After the gig, we had a meeting and she asked me, "What are you doing after the show?" I didn't know. I'm thinking, *Aww shit, here we go!*

But I didn't get lucky…we went out to eat, and we flirted and discussed business. She decided next time she threw an event, she was gonna hire me to do the promotion. She told me she'd put the money up, she'd rent the room, I'd do the promotion and DJ'ing, and we'd split the money fifty-fifty after all the expenses. We did Alpine together and it was a much better turnout. Everything was cool. We made money.

My dad came by my house one day after I had promoted a party at Alpine and saw me counting a pile of money. Now, my house is in a dope-infested area…

"Where you get all this money from?"

"I was DJ'ing at Alpine Village."

"Ain't that much DJ'ing in the damn *world!*"

This was a time when parents had a different attitude about their kids and where and how they got their money. My dad was a hustler with morals, and he was very frugal. He was one generation shy of a share cropper, so manual labor came natural for him.

I didn't want this to be the future make-up of our family, so I decided to do something smarter, and a lot less hard. For me, DJ'ing was my way out. So for him to see me with seven or eight hundred dollars on a Saturday morning—an amount he didn't make all month mowing lawns—was a shock factor for him.

My dad and I had a very tight relationship. He wasn't about to see me go down the wrong path without putting his foot in my ass.

"If I catch you selling dope, I'm kicking your ass out of the house, and kicking your ass again."

"No, dude, I ain't selling no dope. I DJ'd at Alpine Village. I did a promotion last night. I got another one in two weeks; you ought to come by and check it out if you don't believe me."

Eventually, my old man came to one of our teenage dances and we had a good crowd that night. He met Jeannie (he just knew that she and I were a couple) and he saw what I was doing. He was cool with it, but he still wasn't sure.

"Uh-huh, dude, that's risky business. You're a goddamn fool!"

His thing was, it was a good hustle, but his philosophy was, a man needed a good job *and* a good hustle. Caltrans for him was a good job; my DJ'ing at night was a good hustle. I didn't want to do both of 'em. I just wanted to DJ.

Alpine was sold and it went off the grid for a minute. Only a few promoters were allowed to come back. I was one of them. Things were changing.

Fired!

Everything was going along fine at Record Shack for a while, but the day came when my dad's prediction came true. They fired me from Record Shack. Not because I did anything wrong; they fired me because I was successful. It got to the point where I wouldn't even get a paycheck from

Record Shack most of the time. Usually, I would go to the warehouse, pull all the records I needed, give them to the lady in the payroll department, and she'd tally up what I owed and take it out of my pay.

Record Shack paid us in cash. They took our taxes and the whole nine yards, but they paid us in cash. So they took out what I owed for my records, wrote my stub out for my deductions—FICA, SSI, whatever the case may be—and they'd give me the rest of my money in my envelope. It might be as little as $24, $18 sometimes.

They couldn't understand how I could survive off $18. They wondered how I could maintain my style of dress and pay for my semi new Chevy van on as little as $18.00 a week. They came to the conclusion I was doing something that wasn't cool so, just like my dad predicted, they laid me off after only six months in the sales room. I did get vacation pay, the amount they owed me for that week, and the amount they held in the hole, so my final check from Record Shack was about $700. *Now* what in the hell was I supposed to do?

When they fired me, they pulled me into the office and this is pretty much the story they told me:

> "Things have slowed down, and we understand that you're one of the few employees that has an outside source of income that you can fall back on in the event

that you don't have a job here. Nothing personal—we gotta let you go."

"Oh, nothing personal?"

"We gotta let you go."

Okay. I had been there about a year or so (including the time I worked in the warehouse). I took my $700 and walked out of Record Shack. I went home and, boy, talk about a hard conversation! The first person I called was my dad. He kinda gloated, but he still had my back.

7

Lonzo Don't Play That

Before gangsta rap, I had a reputation. I always had to prove myself, because I've always been a mild-mannered person— like to play, like to joke around—and people tend to take my kindness for weakness. That's usually a mistake.

One time, I was working for a promoter and the guy stiffed me for like $75.

> "Here's half your money; I'll give you the other half in a couple of weeks."

Time kept passing and he never did give me my money. So I saw him one day at a club called Total Experience. He pulled up in a Mercedes Benz. Got out of the car and was talking to everybody else. I tapped him on the shoulder.

"Hey man, can I get some part of that $75 you owe me?"

"Oh man, I ain't got no money…" He looked at me, gnarled his teeth and squinted his eyes at me as if to say, "How dare you ask about some money…"

So I quietly pulled him aside.

"Hey dude, when can I get squared away?"

He started talking shit to me. As he got in the car, I was leaning in on the passenger side. His girl was in the car; he was in the driver's seat. Now, I wasn't through with the conversation. I'm kinda on the defensive, feeling guilty because he's acting like I offended him to ask for the money. Then he started talking shit to me in front of the girl.

"Man, fuck you! I ain't givin' you shit!"

I had a slight cold that day. I reached back in my throat and hocked the biggest "luggie" I possibly could and spat right past his girlfriend—hit him dead in the head with it. *Poof!*

"Fuck *you!*

Oh, he was pissed! He got out of the car, pulled off his coat, and came at me. I was backing up go get into position so I could fight him. Somehow, my shoe came off and I stepped on a pebble, and I kinda bent down. By now, I'm totally off balance, waiting for him to kick my ass. I got into a defensive position. Now I'm balled up, waiting for the punch or kick or something, and it never came.

He didn't realize when he came at me that Charles and Fella, my roadies, were in my truck parked right next to the driveway where he was. Charles and Fella were two peas in a pod. Whenever there was a problem, I never had to worry 'bout nobody having my back. They always were there.

They saw us get into it, and as he turned the corner to get to me, one of my guys knocked the SHIT outta him! When I looked up, he was holding *his* head! So of course, I took that as an opportunity to kick his ass a little bit more, and gave him a deadline to pay me my fucking money. I got paid two days later. I didn't know 'til later that he had a reputation for knowing karate, so when word got out that I had kicked his ass, I became known as the DJ not to be messed with.

These are some Disco Lonzo pre-Eve After Dark stories. These stories are part of the evolution of a nonviolent, loving brother who was forced to kick some ass just to survive.

Another time, there were these two brothers in Long Beach who called themselves the IP Promoters (International Promoters). I forgot their names. They loved me. I was a great DJ and they loved me to do all their parties. But they'd only pay me like $150. They were making quite a bit of money.

"Can't I get a bonus or something?"

"Aw man, we ain't got it. We can't do it, Lonzo."

Okay, no problem. Well, a couple of nights when they lost, they asked me for a discount.

"Wait a minute, hold on...when you *made* money two weeks ago, you wouldn't give me no bump. Now you lose money, you want me to give you a discount! No! If ain't no love, ain't no love! That's what you owe me, *that's what you owe me!*"

They got mad, but they knew I was still the best man going. So they did a dance at the Century Plaza Hotel—big, classy hotel in Century City. Great crowd. On this night, they didn't use my sound system; they hired some white boys from out in the valley. White boys came in, set the system up, made sure it worked, and left.

Now these guys decide they wanna play games with my money. I charged them $100 just to DJ. At that time, that

52

was unheard of. $100 and you're not bringing a sound system? *Dude, I need my money!*

My brother Randy and I, we were a team. He looked out for me.

"Randy, go get my money. It's 12 o'clock."

Randy goes to get my money, and they don't have it. Said they'd have it after the set. "After the set" means we're gonna try to fuck you later on. So, I'm in a power position—we got an hour and a half to go. If I hit this switch right now, I still got some power. So I turned the system off.

"What happened to the music?"

"I don't know! I know *nothinnng*! This white boy's shit ain't workin'!"

I sent my brother back to go get my money; this time he came back with the money. I turned the system back on and we got to partying some more. Now they're real pissed at me, so they brought in another DJ after they paid me— my former partner, Rodger Clayton! They took me off the turntable and let Rodger play. So now, I've gotten paid *and* I'm not DJ'ing anymore. I really don't care.

Now they've got it in for me. They hired me about three weeks later to do a gig in Oakland. My brother and I used to always go to their office to meet with these guys. My brother was like 6'3", about 260, 270. He was much bigger than both of these guys. He was like my attack dog. If I didn't like something, he automatically started talking shit. I had to calm him down. That was our routine—good guy, bad guy.

So we go to meet with these guys about the Oakland gig. My brother thought we needed a different approach for this meeting.

"Hey man, in this meeting we need to bring something besides conversation."

"Man, fuck these old punk-ass muthafuckas! They ain't gonna do shit!"

Well, this particular time, as usual, they said something stupid and my brother started talking shit. I don't know where this other guy came from, but the room got dark. We looked up... This cat was about 6'9"—made my brother look like a little baby. The guy walked into the room.

"Everything okay?"

My brother said, "Yeah, it's okay."

We were totally out-manned. These guys and us, we were constantly one-upping each other. They agreed to pay me $500 I think it was, to drive to Oakland and do the gig—$200 up front, and the balance was due at midnight at the gig.

My cousin, my girlfriend and I drive up to Oakland to do the gig—it's an after party for a concert. Unfortunately, the concert went long. The after party didn't happen. They gave me $50 cash and a check for the balance ($250), and told me to cash the check when I got back home.

We load the truck up that night and go straight back to L.A. I go to the bank on Monday morning—no money in the bank. I figure they're not back yet, don't worry about it. I go to the bank on Tuesday—still no money in the bank. I called them on Thursday.

"Hey man, I'm tryin' to get this check cashed so I can get the rest of my money."

"Oh, fuck you! You pulled that shit with us at the Century Plaza, fuck you! We ain't givin' you shit!"

Now, I'm trying to be legal. I go through the legal process, small claims court. They only owe me $250. I get a judgment for $300. I'm trying to collect.

"I got a judgment for $300...can I get $200? We can wrap this thing up right now..."

"Man, fuck you!"

As a young DJ, when I performed I was very, very nervous. My brother told me to take a quarter of a Quaalude. Quaalude is a very relaxing drug. You don't feel high, but you just don't give a damn!

So this day I scraped up some money to pay my truck note, which was a whopping $150 back then. On the way to pay my car note, I dropped that quarter-Quaalude to relax myself. I paid my car note in Long Beach, and these guys' office was in Long Beach, so I got the idea to go by their office and see if I could negotiate with them in person. I got enough gas to get back home.

The brothers did not welcome me with open arms.

"Fuck you! Get the fuck outta my office!"

They called me all kinds of shit. They're sitting in a real estate office. They had the money. This was 1978, and they had brand new LTDs.

They all but ran me out of the office. I was pissed off— scared, but more pissed off than anything. Then that Quaalude kicked in. *Fuck them!*

My brother had used my bumper-jack hammer earlier to fix the battery in his car, and it was in the front seat of my truck. I grabbed that bumper-jack handle and decided, *if you not giving me the money, you're gonna pay the window man.*

I busted every fucking window I could. Headlights, glass, everything. I busted the side windows, tail lights—and when I got to the tail lights, they heard me. Somebody said he was going to get a pistol. Up to this time, I had been very careful not to put my hand through the windshield. When they said they were going to get a pistol, I was just getting to the back windshield.

I refused to run. I put my jack handler through the back window, but this time I did it with so much force, I put my hand through there, too. When I saw them on the porch, I couldn't see what they had in their hand and I didn't want to stick around to find out. I didn't want to get shot. So I snatched my hand out and jumped in my truck.

My truck was a three-speed stick shift on the column—old school. I'm driving home, and as I'm driving I'm talking shit to myself.

"Don't be *fuckin'* with me!"

I'm driving, shifting gears. All of a sudden as I'm shifting, I notice there's blood on the window. *What the fuck? Did I get shot?* I look again, and there's blood on the steering wheel. What happened was when I went through that back window, a huge part of my hand got snatched open. I looked like the terminator. The skin was pulled off—you could see the tendons, the muscles, *everything*. Thank God, thanks to that Quaalude I was very calm. I didn't panic. I made it home, bleeding like a son-of-a-bitch.

My girlfriend Diane took me to Harbor General. They sewed me up. When I got back home, these guys had come to my house. What they didn't realize is that the guys that worked with me lived on the corner. They knew who they were, and they jammed 'em up.

"You lookin' for Lonzo? He ain't here...what's happenin', man?"

Turned out they came to pay me. The next day, I went to their office and got paid in full. Their daddy had told them, "Pay this crazy muthafucka 'fore he kill somebody."

That shit rang throughout the DJ industry for *decades*. That one incident. The bumper jack handle through the windshield was the climax of our relationship. I usually don't burn bridges in business, but that one, I blew the fuck up. They never called me again, and I never called them again. And my reputation as a *crazy* DJ reigned throughout dance promoters.

"Don't fuck with Lonzo and his money. That nigga's crazy!"

From that point on, I had no problems until I got into the club business. I tell all these stories just to say, anybody that knows me knows I'm not a gang banger, not a violent person. But pushed into a corner, I'm gonna come out fighting like any real man would do. But again, I'm not telling these stories to glorify what I did; it's just to verify what I had to go through to be successful in these streets.

You don't run a nightclub on Avalon and El Segundo being no punk. And you don't survive being no flashy-ass hoodlum—somebody's gonna challenge your ass and they're gonna be a little bit tougher than you are. So you have to learn to walk the median.

Old School Party Promotions

Nowadays, most promoting is done through social media. Today, everybody can grab some colored fliers, put them on YouTube and Facebook, and pass a few of them out in the club. But back then, there was no social media. Back then, it was hard work. We'd have to hang up 300 posters minimum just for the club on Friday and Saturday night, which meant it would cost you about $200 just to hang them, not including the cost of the posters.

I'd send out about eight guys going in four different directions with hammers and nails about an inch and a half long with the cork back—they were roofing nails. And this way, when the posters went on the poles, it wasn't easy to snatch them down. They did this usually for about a two to five mile radius around the club or any event that we had. That was our main source of advertising, along with fliers.

If you wanted to start a fight with a promoter, snatch his poster down. This was physical labor. You got guys out there starting at about midnight when traffic dies down. They're running across the street in rain, sleet or snow, hanging up posters on telephone poles, and my job the next day was I'd ride around and see what they did the night before. If I rode down the street and didn't see my posters, I didn't wanna pay people!

If they couldn't get paid, and there was somebody else's posters in a spot where they knew they had hung mine, they would go knock on the door or find out where their business was...it would be a serious problem! I mean, we weren't gang-bangers, but you had to respect the posters. We didn't shoot nobody or nothing like that. We didn't stab anybody, but we *would* whip your ass.

It was understood that nobody would snatch your posters off the poles. Our posters would stay up because Eve After Dark was an every week event. But also, we had a certain kind of poster. Every other week or so, we would change colors, and certain posters went up in certain territories that we had. You didn't snatch them down. These were our weekly posters—don't snatch them down, because you *will* get your ass whipped.

Today's fliers are quarter-sheet, full color back and front glossy. Back in the day, we had one sheet of paper, a full sheet of paper—no gloss, no color, just black and white.

My boy Darryl Davis was our graphics guy. Darryl and I were laughing recently about how things have changed so much in our lifetime. When I was brought up, there was no computer on everybody's desk. There was no Internet. This stuff did not exist when I was coming up. We were laughing about some of the ways he did his fliers, and my boy Dale Manner who had the print shop…he was a major player. Dale printed fliers for everybody.

8

Eve After Dark

After my dad saw me at the Alpine and after I got laid off from Record Shack, he talked to his friend Jefty Harris about what I was doing. His club was named Jefty's. Jefty and my dad were best friends. Jefty was a contractor and my dad was a landscaper, so they did work together, plus Jefty's was my dad's drinking hangout. Jefty had just built a second story on his club in 1977. It was having little to no success at that time, and my old man suggested to Jefty that he give me an opportunity based on my success at Alpine.

Jefty is 6'4", got a very deep voice, and his facial expression is always like he's mad. Nice guy, but he looked like he was always mad. My dad brought me to him. I was twenty-one years old. I was fucking *terrified* to walk up the stairs to what is my office right now. Jefty trusted my old man's opinion. My dad walked me to the office (this is thirty-some-odd years ago), sat me down on the other side of the same desk I'm sitting at right now, and turned me over to Jefty.

"Look man, my son wants to be in the entertainment business. He's giving dances at Alpine Village. He gets a good crowd; he's making money. If you want to do something, you gotta do it right, and I figure if anybody can teach him how to do it, you can. I told him he might want to come over and check you out and see if you guys can make some money together."

Jefty's deep voice announced the warning.

"Lookit, goddammit, if I give you an opportunity and you fuck me, I'm gonna kick your ass, understood?"

And then my dad chimes in.

"If he has to kick your ass, you got *two* ass kickin's coming. He has permission to kick your ass, and if he has to kick your ass, I'ma kick your ass for making him have to kick your ass and making me look bad."

This is how they talked to me! So I'm sitting there thinking, *what have I got myself into?* With the warning out of the way, Jefty gave me the rules.

"I don't want no dope in my club. I don't want this, I don't want that, and the first time I have any of these problems here, your ass is gone."

I was under pressure walking in the door! I talked to my buddy Rodger.

"Hey man, I got a chance to do this spot at this club over on Avalon and El Segundo…you want a piece of it?"

"Oh **hell** no, man, that's sherm-head territory! Hell no, you can have that—I don't wanna fuck with that. I don't want no parts of that."

What Rodger didn't realize was that I'm *from* this sherm-head infested area, born and raised, all my life. I knew all the sherm-heads. I knew dudes that sold the sherm. I knew everybody. Anyway, he turned it down, so I reluctantly went to Jeannie.

"Look, I got an opportunity to do something, do you want in?"

"Sure! What do we need?"

"It's probably gonna take us about $1100 to get started."

That was the beginning of Eve After Dark. Jefty charged us $600 a week, $300 a night. Plus we had to put advertisements together. I was passing out flyers. Jeannie was here from the very beginning and she financed my start. It didn't take off right away. She'd give me $1100 on Monday; I gave Jefty his money and gave Jeannie her money on Sunday. I'd still be broke on Monday.

We opened at Eve After Dark in June of 1979—June 22nd, to be exact. Rappers Delight came out in that same time period, and Eve After Dark opened along with Parliament Funkadelic dropping "Knee Deep." All that shit happened at the same time. And we were passing out fliers and kinda stumbling along our way. We were doing okay, not great. I could pay our few bills and keep Jefty happy, and Jeannie was getting her money. Everything was cool.

Shortly after I opened the Eve, I met Lewis Harper. He ran a record pool called the R&B Disco Truth. At that time, Lewis was the promotional director for Arista Records. Lewis would hang at the Eve to see the response to the records he was promoting. We eventually became friends. One day he called and I had to pick him up at Jheryl Busby's office. He introduced me to Jheryl Busby, who was also his brother-in-law at the time.

Jheryl Busby was probably one of the most powerful Black men in the record industry next to Berry Gordy and guys like that. He was in that league. He asked Lewis if he had any appearances for Cameo—they had a new song out ("Shake Your Pants"). Cameo was one of the hottest groups of

1979. That was when groups went to clubs to promote their songs. So I'm sitting in the office, and I'm excited.

"Bring 'em to my club, man!"

Jheryl asked, "What club you got?"

"Eve After Dark on Avalon and El Segundo. It's pretty cool."

"Okay, they can go down there."

I went to KDAY the next day. I bought ten commercials on KDAY. Ten 10-second spots. "Tonight at Eve After Dark, Avalon and El Segundo, Cameo live." That's all the commercial said. Ten times cost me a hundred dollars. It was $10 a spot.

So Jheryl sent Cameo down to the Eve. Cameo packed the joint out, and the cold part about it was, if you know anything about Cameo, the original Cameo back in the day was a nine-piece group. That's when they had the band and horn section all traveling together. Cameo just sent the horn section, but their faces were on the posters and flats, and that's all the folks needed.

That night Eve was on fire, packed to capacity. "Shake Your Pants" had the crowd moving. That night, Eve After Dark took off like never before. *My God,* we were off the chain! You gotta understand, this is the first time I ever made over $2,000 in my life by myself. It was a Thursday night. I still had Friday and Saturday to make some money, and I did. We never looked back after that.

Anthony "AK" King remembers…

"Eve After Dark was the Black Disneyland of the Ghetto! I mean, we built our confidence with each other there—girls, too! Girls knew where the boys were gonna be, so they could wear their new whatever was in style. We didn't care, we just liked girls! It was a platform for us to develop into some really incredible people."

While we were enjoying our success, my now cross-town rival Rodger was building up steam with his crew, Uncle Jamm's Army. Rodger and his boys came to me about five months after we got the Eve rolling and tried to get in on what had become the hottest spot in the city. Andre, aka "Unknown DJ," who was head of promotions and music and my right hand man, politely—in his very dry but humorous way—told them to kiss his *and* my ass.

There was no place like Eve After Dark. Eve After Dark was the only teen club in the city, with the exception of the Workshop on 91st and Western. It was located near, but not in, Compton—technically about a quarter mile out of Compton—but we got a lot of support from Compton and Watts residents.

Days of Style

We were always dressed to the T. We wore slacks. We wore dress shirts. We were clean every day. That was the difference between today and back in the day. We had a different dress code; we had a different look. We had a different feel. We had a different vibe.

Back then, we didn't wear tennis shoes on a regular basis. Tennis shoes were something you did when you went to go play basketball. I recall playing football in dress shoes and slacks—*because we could!* If you ever see New Jack City, you'll see Gene Money playing basketball. He would take his shirt off; he was bare-chested, and he was playing basketball in slacks and dress shoes. That was a sign of a real hustler back then.

Because Eve was located in the County of Los Angeles, it didn't fall under the rules of L.A. City or Compton, so we were able to do things in that area that at that time L.A. and Compton didn't allow, one of which was staying open until 5 a.m. and DJ'ing. If the crowd was still big, people could hang out at my club until about 6 a.m. We had the young clientele because we didn't have any alcohol. We were allowed to let people in as young as sixteen, but we advertised eighteen and over. After midnight or 1 a.m., it became an after-hours joint for all the young twenties to early thirties who didn't want to go to Carolina West.

We were unique in having after hours. This was possible mainly because back in the day, L.A. County had different rules from L.A. City. The City had a law that stated no jukeboxes, no singing, and no live entertainment. But The Crew and I were determined to keep the club open after hours, so we found a loophole in the law—they never stated no DJs. Everything was going perfectly. We opened at 10 p.m. and closed at 6 a.m.

We had everything going smooth for three years, but a bump came when things started to get redundant. So being the geniuses that we were, we hired a three-piece in-house band who called themselves Sundance, Green Eyes and Black just to keep things fresh. The main purpose was for us to rap in front of the crowd, but that only worked for about three weeks.

After that I had a new plan—I wanted to make a record. I thought it would blow up like Run-DMC. So we headed to the studio and did the basic drum beats, kick drums and a scratch record. The type of sound Run-DMC would make. It had vocals by Cli-N-Tel and the scratch was by Yella. This record only took forty-five minutes to create. It sold just about 2,500 copies locally, and kicked off of our record career.

We also made a song called The E-A-D rap, but because on every record they had a federal copyright imprint, I was scared that if we didn't get a clearance, the FBI would track us down and take us to jail. Meanwhile, the Eve was rocking and I was putting money aside to go into the studio.

9

Young Baller

I was balling out of control

I had the same problem that so many youngsters had in the rap industry: I had a pile of money at a young age. I was a power player in my own head. I walked around wearing my name, "Lonzo," in gold. Had a little razor under the "Lonzo." I'd take the razor off and cut up my little cocaine and shit like that. I thought I was the shit. The only thing I had that most kids didn't have, especially in the record industry—I had a dad and a club owner that both were gonna kick my ass at the same time if I stepped out of line!

At this time back in the day, I kept fifty grand in a stash box. Fifty thousand! At one point, I had a *hundred* thousand dollars cash money stashed! At twenty-three years old, I had a hundred thousand dollars cash money. Didn't know what to *do* with it! I had a live-in girlfriend. *She* didn't know what was there! How did I manage not to let her know about that? I paid attention to good advice…

When I was paying Jefty his rent each week, I couldn't just give him his money. No, I had to sit down and get a lecture. And that weekly lecture sometimes was alcohol-induced, but nonetheless, it was informative to no end. I tried to slide in and slide out, but I couldn't do it. Jefty's about 6'4", a big guy.

"Sit down!" he'd say. "Have a seat. How's everything going? What you doing with your money?"

He was concerned. It wasn't about me just making the money, it was about me making money and doing something with it, not being stupid. He was always looking over my shoulder. He didn't understand what I was doing, how I was getting it done, because he came from a different era.

Nonetheless, he let me do my thing with the understanding that once I made some money, I had to pay it forward and help somebody else come up as well. That combined with my Catholic school training and hanging around with my dad, who was an open-hearted person, made me a giver. I watched my dad give literally 'til it hurt him, cosigning for cars and things of that nature. He just was a great-hearted person, so I got that from him.

So Jefty would not let me just pay him and walk out of the office. It wasn't that kind of party for him. He would sit me down and we would have a heart to heart talk. He saw I was having some success and he would talk to me about my money—don't do this with my money, don't do that with it, don't put it there, the tax man is gonna clean me out if I don't have a tax deduction… He schooled me on how to take care of my business. Taught me to keep my mouth shut. At twenty-three years old.

"Don't tell nobody the kind of money you're makin', fool! Somebody's liable to kick your door down and hurt your ass! And don't be flashy!"

73

I took most of what he said to heart, except for the flashy part. I always liked to dress, even before I got to the Eve, so having a few dollars, a bunch of girls around, and being the boss at an early age, I had to look the part. At that time, I'm wearing suits every day at the club; every Friday I got a suit. I always liked to be clean. Now I got a reason to be clean, but Jefty had other advice.

> "Stop wearing them damn suits and carrying your briefcase! Stop carrying the goddamn briefcase, 'cause somebody's gonna think that's where you keep money and they're gonna knock you in the head!"

Jefty gave me insights to things that I didn't understand at that time, but now that I'm fifty-eight years old, *Ohhhh, okay, I see what you were talking about!* And I see why it's so important that older men stay in the community, because that's knowledge that has to be recycled.

> "When you make yourself some money, you cannot be chicken-shit and not give back," Jefty told me. "I've given to you; you gotta give to somebody else."

That was one of his requirements—when you get some money, you gotta keep the chain going, you can't stop it.

Jefty taught me a lot of knowledge that you can't get in a book. Sometimes we talked for forty-five minutes, sometimes we talked for three hours! And I'd sit there and listen. Sometimes I didn't want to hear what he had to say, but today I'm glad I did. I would not trade those lessons for anything else in the world.

10

East Rocks West

After doing pop lock contests and various forms of local live entertainment, I decided to bring in recording acts like Run DMC and Kurtis Blow. That was a very interesting time because it was the first time we really saw the cultural differences between New York and the West Coast.

I brought in Run DMC probably somewhere around June or July. At that time, my crew and I traveled in packs—wherever I went, usually two or three guys went with me. So Dr. Rock or Yella or whoever, we're all in the van and we go to the airport to pick up Run DMC.

These guys got on leather pants, leather hats and tennis shoes, and we got on baggy pants and skinny ties—we look like Morris Day and the Time and they look like outlaw bikers! There was an immediate culture shock for both of us! Those New York guys wore leather suits the whole time they were here—off the plane, at sound check, on stage—they were here like three, maybe four days, and I never saw them in anything but those leather suits.

"Wherever y'all came from in New York, it must have been awful cold, but it ain't cold in L.A.!"

We dropped them off at the hotel. We didn't hang out at all. I was still promoting the gig. I only remember hanging out with one, and it was after the show—that was Jam Master J. He and I hit it off pretty cool. I don't remember any real interaction with Run or DMC—we were cool, but what pissed me off with them was that as part of their show, they threw the microphone down! Broke my damn mic! I was mad as a muthafucka! I only had two mic's and you broke one of 'em doing your show...I'm like, *come on, man!* I didn't trip too much, but again, I didn't like that shit!

After the show, Jam Master J and I kicked it for a minute. He was different, more interactive. Asked more questions. He wanted a forty-ounce, so I took him around to the local liquor store, bought him a forty-ounce, came back to the club, he knocked it off in the office or whatever, and we just jelled a lot easier.

We talked about upcoming projects. Nobody knew shit yet. I was trying to pick his brain; he didn't know shit either. Everybody was new to this shit. Nobody had any real inside info, no major success yet. It was like the blind leading the blind.

Two days later, they were performing at one of Rodger's events. Again, I was pissed off.

11

History of
the Wrecking Crew

A little Wrecking Crew history: The *original* members of the recording group with the original name Wrecking Crew were the club's first DJ's: Sweet Ron Ron out of New York, Billy T out of Sacramento, my buddy from around the corner, Dr. Rock (he eventually became a very popular radio DJ in Texas), and also Andre, the Unknown DJ. I met Billy and Ron Ron when I was dealing with Lewis Harper in an R&B Disco Truth record pool, which was a big asset when it came to the success of Eve After Dark. The five of us were the 1979 DJs of Eve After Dark. All of those guys moved on except Unknown; he left before we started recording legitimate records; he started his own record label—Techno Hop.

Now on my second go round, it was just the cleanup guys and the promoters that were the Wrecking Crew. We didn't become Wreckin' Cru right away because we didn't become recording stars right away. An attorney for a group out in the Midwest sent us a Cease and Desist letter because that group already had the name "Wrecking Crew." This was during the 1984 Olympics and I kept hearing "world class this" and "world class that," so I asked my attorney if I added World Class, dropped the "ing" and changed Crew to Cru, would that be sufficient. He said yes, so that's how we became the World Class Wreckin' Cru.

A new guy joined the Crew—a Dr. Rock fan, DJ Yella. Then I met Cli-N-Tel in a rap contest at the Eve After Dark. Unknown was always around; I'd known him for years, even before I got the club. He was around when I was just starting to make cassettes at home. I met Unknown and Rodger Clayton at the Long Beach Convention Center when I was doing that gig for IP Promoters. Unknown still to this day thinks I met him somewhere else.

Dre was the last member to come on board. He came to my attention through a partner of mine named Timmy "Smokey" Gamble (R.I.P.) from the neighborhood. Tim was one of the cleanup guys with Charles "Fat Fat" Queens, and he wanted me to meet this guy from around the corner who was kicking ass on the turntables. Oddly enough, I knew all of Dre's people but not Dre; he was eight years younger than me.

Part III

The Wreckin' Cru Introductions

Meet the DJs that changed the world.

12

Andre "Dr. Dre" Young

Calling Dr. Dre to Surgery

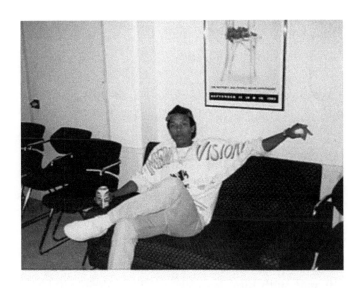

1983. The Eve After Dark is crackin'. I went downstairs to check on my security guards and make sure everything was straight. These two young guys walk up—a tall guy and a short guy. Because I had an age limit, they couldn't come in, plus they weren't dressed right. I tried to keep older-looking teens. I wanted the Eve to look like "Soul Train" and not "Romper Room." That night, Dre and Eazy looked and dressed young.

I hear Dre talking to his short partner.

"I know him, that's my uncle's friend."

"Who are you?" I asked.

"I'm Andre."

"Andre who?"

"You know my people, man, the Young's—Debra and Lloyd and Floyd and Teddy…"

"Okay, yeah, I know who you are. What's up with you? How you doing, man?"

"I wanna come in the club!"

"Well dude, you're a little young, plus you're not dressed right, but since I know your folks, if you wanna come in, you tighten up your clothes and you can come on in."

Eazy E was with him; he was still Eric Wright then. Eric started talking shit.

"Aw man, this is Eve After Dark, I ain't gotta get fuckin' dressed to come up in here."

A week or so later, Dre shows back up, got a little skinny tie on and baggy pants. At that time, the clothing flavor of the day was Morris Day and the Time for the guys—baggy pants, skinny ties and shirts. Dre comes up and he's dressed to the T. I let Dre in. Eazy wasn't happy.

"What about me?"

"You still dressed like a bum! You can't come in here."

People wore the Jheri curl at that time, but Eric still had a natural.

"Yeah, ya Jheri curl Morris Day looking..."

Askia remembers...

"Andre ["Dre"] was an introvert...a very quiet, inward type of person. To me, it is amazing to see the phenomenon of him in gangsta rap with his personality. That whole attitude was fabricated to promote a different attitude in the community. That was not his background.

"I've seen Andre maybe two or three times over the years. I'll see him and call out, 'Andre!' and he'll

83

get out of the limo because he knows whoever calls him Andre knows him. And he'll give me a hug... 'Hey Askia, how you doin'?' He knows that I know him. I knew him as a silly kid. They were kids— nineteen or twenty. None of 'em came from this particular background at all. Nothing hard-core. They didn't even have that type of mannerism in their behavior.

"When Lonzo formed the Wreckin' Cru, it was a youthful movement—young ones just havin' party time, havin' a good time. It started out very innocent. Wreckin' Cru was formed of local talent. Dre just happened to be in the neighborhood. Antoine ("Yella") just happened to be in the neighborhood..."

I had heard about Dre from one of the boys in the neighborhood, but I didn't put two and two together. My boy Timmy ("Smokey") Gamble worked for me. He kept telling me about Dre.

So Dre's in the club and he's hanging out. All of a sudden, after about thirty-five or forty minutes, I don't know how he did it to this day, but I looked up at the turntable and my guys weren't up there. **Dre** was up there! He was mixing two records—*Please Mr. Postman* and a song called *Planet Rock*! We had never heard two records being mixed together this way before. One's R&B, one's a dance cut,

84

and the tempos matched up because one is half the speed of the other. They worked together. Nobody had ever heard this done before and the people stopped dancing just to look. There was a lot of, *"Wow, what is this?"*

I saw that the guy had some talent, and when he got through, I talked to him.

"Hey, what else you got?

"Aw man, I got a few other things I can do..."

By this time, I'm also making my bootleg mixed 12-inches. DJ Yella was my mix guy at the time. My friend and business partner, Andre aka the Unknown DJ, had recruited Dre before I did and put him on his team for mixes. We both made mixed 12-inches, and it was always a fight for new music.

I noticed two things about Dre. One—he liked to be clean, and two—he loved women, I admired his skill with ladies. He was the ultimate player. Another thing I noticed about Dre—later when he was recording in my studio, guess what the number one thing was that I had to buy over and over because Dre kept fucking them up? Headphones. Muthafuckin' headphones! Dre would get in the studio and get to grooving, phone would ring, he'd run over to the phone with the headphones on, and fuck the cord up. Damn—*I'm* the one gotta buy some more headphones.

So Dre's mixing for Unknown and Yella's mixing for me, but because I have all the connections with the record stores, I'm getting the most money. I'm the King of this right here. Something happened two months later—Dre wasn't happy with Unknown. Now he's coming to work for me, doing mixes for me. Shortly after that, the mixing business kinda fell apart because everybody and his mama started doing the same thing and it kinda got diluted. We moved on to legitimate records.

Dre's favorite rapper was LL Cool J. When we did our song "House Calls," Shakespeare told Dre he sounded like LL Cool J and gave him the nickname LL Cool Dre.

Shakespeare Recalls…

"I remember how when we would get back off tour, because Dre was a popular DJ back then, a lot of guys would approach him about doin' these mixes, especially Steve Yano. Andre would do a lot of mixes for Steve and Lonzo would be upset and tried to explain it to Dre.

'Hey man, listen—you are a popular DJ, man, in the Wreckin' Cru, signed to a major record company. At least you oughta be gettin' paid for the work that you're doing!'

"Dre's thing at that time was like he really didn't care about the money, it was for the love of doin' his craft. But then as time went on, people started gettin' in his ear and created a little monster…"

Fail to Bail

Right before we signed with CBS, I bought a BMW 633. Dre begged me to sell him my Mazda RX7. I lied to the finance company (told them I was Dre's uncle), which allowed me to cosign for him to buy the car from me.

Now we're signed to CBS, our release date has been pushed back to July, no gigs, and we're running out of money. I'm paying my car note *and* Dre's car note, I'm getting him out of jail, *and* we're not gigging. It got to the point where Dre was borrowing money from me and I was still paying his car note. Dre had a bad habit of getting speeding tickets. He had been to jail two or three times, and the third time he called me, I had to convey some tough love.

"Hey man, I'm not getting you out this time. We ain't giggin' right now. We ain't got nowhere to go. Sit your ass in jail for a couple days, you'll stop gettin' these speeding tickets!"

"Oh my God! Oh no! Man I gotta get out of jail! I can't stay in jail!"

Somehow or other, Eric was contacted and he bailed Dre out, with the understanding that once he bailed him out, he would do some beats for him. That was the beginning of his deal with Eric. Dre's pissed at me because I did not run to his rescue. Eric's in his ear about working on his projects. So he, in turn, cuts the deal to do the production.

13

Antoine "DJ Yella" Carraby

Eve After Dark had been open about two years. Yella came through as a regular customer and kinda hung out watching Dr. Rock, one of my main jocks, learning his style. When Dr. Rock moved to Texas, DJ Yella slid in.

Yella joined the Crew under the name of Bric Hard and was first a DJ, then he was a promoter helping pass out flyers. He started out mixing for me. The name Yella came out of Unknown DJ calling him a piss-colored son-of-a-bitch (he was joking about something Yella said), and from then on everybody called him Yella.

Yella seemed damn near bipolar. He was a total introvert around people. *Total* introvert. I mean, he could be in a room and you'd never know he was there. But, he was a drum major for Compton High School. Once he got going, he wouldn't shut up, but you gotta get him going. He was always the most pessimistic cat I've ever met in my life. He didn't believe in anything. He didn't believe in himself, he didn't believe in me…

"Aw man, that ain't gonna happen."

I mean he was Al Bundy! Always telling me what I couldn't do. And for me, that's fuel for the fire. As soon as you tell me I can't do it, *oh shit*, now I got to prove you wrong.

With Yella, I always had to give him pep talks, keep him reinforced, keep the fire lit. He and Dre would eventually become competitors to see how many women they could sleep with at various points in time.

At the other extreme, Yella was a cheapskate to no end. He wrote phone numbers on the back of other people's business cards. He'd have a *stack* of business cards. If he wanted to find somebody's number, he would thumb through all those business cards 'til he found the number. That was his thing. He had a couple of other jobs.

Shakespeare remembers...

"One of the guys in the group, Antoine Carraby (DJ Yella), was idolizing Prince back then. I remember when we had signed this deal, we went to go get some costumes and we ended up going down Melrose. Everybody was pickin' out their costumes, and of course Yella picked up some paisley stuff."

Yella became part of the Wreckin' Crew. Through the ups and downs, he gained notoriety with us. When it came to costumes, everybody else had some manly looking shit and Yella would get lace gloves and Prince shit, the little one-eye thing with the lace bandana and shit. Yella always wanted to be fucking Prince. We would be on stage and this muthafucka would stick his finger in his mouth and do all the little Prince moves. I'm like, *muthafucka will you just do your goddamn part?!*

14

Marquette "Cli-N-Tel" Hawkins

Cli-N-Tel was a smart cat. He was in the 12th grade at Centennial when I met him. He worked in a library and some more places. He was the last member to join the group, and also the first one to leave.

Of the Wreckin' Cru, Cli-N-Tel was the only one that had a college degree. Only one. I don't have a college degree. I went to college…didn't finish. Dre and Yella came to me fresh out of high school.

I met Cli-N-Tel at a rap contest I had at the Eve. He kicked ass so hard in that contest that when I decided to make my first record, I wanted him to be the lead on it. He's a very articulate rapper.

I hated to see him go. He always tried to understand the business; always tried to understand what I was trying to do. But he got some serious misinformation from my former manager (Shirley) and didn't get over it; he left the group and later was the first one to sue me. Cli-N-Tel left after World Class Wreckin' Cru's debut album, "World Class."

Even after all that, we're still cool to this day. Cli-N-Tel and I are talking about getting together with Shakespeare and Mona to hit the road again and maybe record a new project. We're looking forward to seeing what the future holds.

15

Barry "Shakespeare" Severe

When we signed with Epic Records (part of CBS), Shakespeare was now the lead MC.

Shakespeare was never a part of Eve After Dark. He came in after Eve and Dooto's, and only joined us on tour.

While we were signed to Epic, our executive producer, Larkin Arnold, asked me if I had another group. I wasn't sure since they weren't actually signed to me yet, but I mentioned Stereo Crew. Stereo Crew consisted of Ice Cube, K-Dee, Jinx and Shakespeare. After some thought, I decided to bring Shakespeare into Wreckin' Cru and signed the younger guys to CBS as Stereo Crew. CBS gave Stereo Crew a single deal with an option for an album, and gave Wreckin' Cru an album deal.

When I think back on Shakespeare's career with Wreckin' Cru, I always think of a Mark Wahlberg movie, "Rock Star." The group in the movie was called the Steel Dragons. Shakespeare came into an already established Wreckin' Cru and fit like a glove. We had plenty of fans and we were doing our thing. Being from the streets, Shakespeare always had my back if we had any problems on the road. He was usually the voice of reason. He'd try to talk me down, being somewhat of the spiritual leader of the group. Before we hit the stage, he always led us in prayer; he's a preacher right to this day.

Shakespeare recalls...

"It was interesting the way I got into the Wreckin' Cru. I was in O'Shea's (Ice Cube's) group. During

this time when we were going to the studio just trying to put together some tracks, 1580 KDAY—a popular hip hop radio station back then—they were doing a **Best Rapper in the West** *contest. We entered the contest and we made it all the way to the finals.*

"By that time, Sir Jinx (coincidentally, Dr. Dre's cousin) had already introduced us to Lonzo and everybody that was in the group. Lonzo was already in negotiations at that time with CBS Records to sign his group, the World Class Wreckin' Cru, and another group to the label.

"We ended up taking 2nd place in the **Best Rapper in the West** contest. A couple of companies had made us some offers but we really didn't entertain 'em 'cause we already knew that we were going with Lonzo and the Wreckin' Cru. He was gonna sign us and be our producer.

"At that time when all this was going on, one of the members of the Wreckin' Cru, Cli-N-Tel, had got upset after somebody gave him some misinformation regarding money, so he ended up leaving the group right when they were getting ready to go on tour, and so Lonzo made an offer to me.

"It was the opportunity of a lifetime to be in the Wreckin' Cru—they already were local celebrities.

They had already put out an album. So I told my group what the deal was, and they were like, hey man, go for it. So I jumped at the opportunity.

"In the beginning it was great being around Lonzo's house and in the studio. It was the buzz. Everybody wanted to come through and be a part of it. The shows that we were doing—even though we were a rap group, we were doing soul with groups like Atlantic Starr, the Bar-Kays, Shirelle, Alexander O'Neal, Morris Day.

"At that time, we were hot because Lonzo was really death on us rehearsing and having our choreography down. We were like New Edition, where we had the lyrics, the costumes, the choreography—get away from the mic and go right back to the mic and get your part..."

16

The Jackets

In the Wreckin' Cru, once you proved yourself to be a worthy member, you were qualified to get one of the most coveted items of the eighties…a Wreckin' Cru jacket. If you had a Wreckin' Cru jacket, you were probably one of the most envied cats in the south central Compton area.

I got the idea for the jacket from my record company buddies. All record companies back in the day had satin jackets. I found out where they got their jackets made, and I wanted the same thing for my fellas.

I bought four of them for the guys in the group, and everybody else started crying and talking about "I want one." So now we got about twenty cats with jackets, and they were reversible.

One side was silver, one side was burgundy. The silver side didn't have any markings on it. Most of the time at a party, we'd flip them around. Oh my God, talk about an uproar! And we had girls wearing these jackets, too!

My boy had me laughing the other day.

"Man, you's a gang leader!"

I'm not a gang leader! I was a leader of an organization of promoters, and at that time, Wreckin' Cru was a big dog. Uncle Jamm's Army was big, too, but we were just as big if not bigger, because we gave dances EVERY week, Friday and Saturday, for about seven years! They gave bigger dances—they had five or six thousand people in a room at one time at the Sports Arena—but we did it consistently on a weekly basis.

Nobody else did what we did. Nobody else had a standing order at the poster shop for posters every week. Nobody had the relationship with the radio stations like I had. My sales rep from thirty years ago and I are still friends today! Rochelle—that's my sales rep from KDAY from 1982— still sells me advertisements today while she works for KJLH. In fact, it was Rochelle who introduced me to Greg Mack (soon to be known as "The Mack Attack"). So the relationships that we had with people stuck.

17

Early Days

When we created Slice, it was after the bootleg stage. We were now creating legitimate records. Surgery was the first record we did that got real recognition, mainly because more production was involved.

We hired this guy by the name of Daniel Soffer, a local musician that owned a complete Oberheim system, DMX drum machine, DSX sequencer and an OB8 keyboard—this was the Rolls Royce of digital music production systems—to do the beats for this record.

We made "Slice" in '83. That was DJ Yella. My whole plan was to make a rap record about each member of the Wreckin' Cru.

"Slice"

"SLICE" "YELLA"

MASTER-ROCKERS

"Rap By D.J. Clientele!"

DJ Yella was a major part of me putting things together. He would do mobile DJ parties at high schools. I would book parties—proms, after-proms, noon dances, homecoming dances, whatever the case may be. Charged x-amount of bucks, paid him to do the gig, and took the profit from those events and put it to the side to buy equipment. One of the ways I paid him back for being so cool about doing the gigs was by doing our first record about him.

Shortly after that, Dre joined the Cru and we did "Surgery," and those dudes tried to convince me to say that we were from Carson or Gardena or something like that. That was very first time I had to make an executive decision that caused a major rift between us—we were *from* Compton and we were *claiming* Compton!

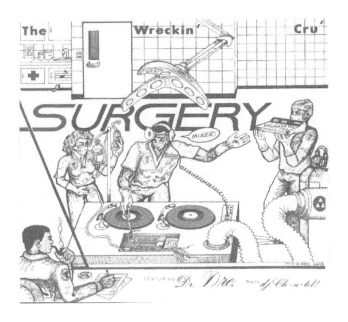

We ended up doing a couple more records about Dre. One was "Housecalls." The other one was "He's Bionic." So we ended up doing three records about Dre. Having "Dr." attached to Dre's name gave us a lot more creative leeway than we had using "Lonzo" or "Shakespeare."

Shakespeare...

"The studio was great because Lonzo had it state-of-the-art for that time and it had a place where we could rehearse. Everything was built right in. As a matter of fact, when we signed the deal with CBS and went into the

studio, the studio Lonzo had in the back of the house was so good that when we sat down with Larkin Arnold, he listened to the tracks and he was like, 'Okay man, where is the master so we can go on and lock this up!' Lonzo told him, 'Man, them is just demo's right there.' Larkin almost fell outta his office chair 'cause he couldn't believe that those were demo tracks. That's just how good the equipment was and everything.

"It was a good time back then...always different local groups trying to come through the studio back then. These guys wanted what we had. That even, in turn, created like a little friendly rivalry between us and L.A. Dream Team.

*"Later on we left CBS and came back to Kru-Cut Records. That was during the time Andre did a project with a rap group called HBO for **Boyz in the Hood**."*

We had to have showmanship to survive against the R&B acts back then because we were the only rap act on the bill. And restrictions for recording were so different back then also. When we did "Housecalls" and he said, "Dre, now I know who you are, I'ma kick you're a—." Couldn't even say the "ss"! We had to cut it off at 'a' because the restrictions for speaking were so damn tight, just the thought of him saying 'ass' was like unheard of! That goes to show you how much things have changed.

Dre and Yella kinda shared the DJ responsibilities. Sometimes one was the focus DJ, sometimes the other one was. When we gigged, Dre would be the DJ and Yella would run the equipment. Sometimes Yella would DJ and Dre would be out front while Shakespeare and I did lyrics, depending on what song it was.

Everybody had their various roles, but for some reason Dre ended up getting most of the attention. Oddly enough, somehow or other we never got around to *my* record.

One day we got a phone call while promoting Dooto's. I was surprised to get this phone call. They wanted us to perform at Vortex up in Sacramento. We were not prepared, but we went anyway. Rented a U-Haul truck. My cousin Joel drove.

Fat Fat was the roadie. Fat Fat was a street smart kid; he climbed under the U-Haul truck and disconnected the odometer so we didn't have to pay mileage.

Vortex was cool. This was the first gig that made me want to get in the record business even more. Now we're getting paid $1,500 with no expenses other than travel. $1,500 to $2,000 a night and just pay my crew; no initial cash layout.

Vortex totally opened my eyes to the potential of what we had stumbled into. Made more sense for me to start gigging than to keep promoting events!

By the time we got back home from Vortex, the phone was ringing for us to go to Texas, Louisiana…like wow, what happened? Got real cool real fast.

Thanks to Greg Mack, the record actually got airplay—that was such a big difference. Everything was going great. We were getting more and more attention and the record was getting more order requests. That may not sound like an issue, but when you have more orders than you have money to manufacture the records, you're kinda screwed.

At that time we were dealing with Bill Smith Custom Records located in El Segundo, CA. This was a C.O.D. company—cash on delivery—since I needed 30 days to get my money back.

Askia ...

> *"We often create things and don't realize how much of an impact it might have on the world. Lonzo was makin' a living, he was makin' some money. I don't think he ever wondered, 'Am I creating something that's gonna become international?'"*

The World Class Wreckin' Cru had a good run. For a good while, we were having a ball. We were on the road, just the four of us living it up—Myself, Dre, Yella, and Cli-N-Tel. By this time, Surgery and Juice had started the phone ringing. We started performing up in northern California—Sacramento, Frisco, Fresno, etc. By the time we got home, a gig was waiting for us in Texas and Louisiana. Life was pretty good for the Wreckin' Cru.

Askia...

> *"I was seeing this phenomenon in my cousin's club, so I really didn't know the impact it was having around the country. There was one particular time when Lonzo had a show in Sacramento. I was taken aback by the amount of attendance at that event! I was accustomed to the Wreckin' Cru at Jefty's local club, and to find that it had crossed over and this music had spread to other parts of the country was unique. It gave me another impression of what really was goin' on. I didn't know how big this rap*

107

music was, and to see this new art form developing and see the young ones really embracing it…

"Lonzo not only had the club, but he would put together dances. You had other segments. Lonzo had the Wreckin' Cru. A guy named Rodger had Uncle Jamm's Army. Larry Grisby and them formed LSD. They were all doing their little dances around the city. I had to realize inside myself that there was some impact developing."

By the time we finished doing some gigs up in Oakland and the surrounding area, Surgery and Juice were released. The Wreckin' Cru had just finished doing a run with Doug E Fresh, UTFO and the Rappin' Duke. While we were on our way back home, LL Cool J had just released "I Need Love," so Cli-N-Tel and I decided that we needed to do a ballad.

We ended up creating "Lovers," which was our first ballad and our first record that was not a dance tune. It was on our "World Class" album it was patterned after a 70's hit "Float on" by the floaters. It was our biggest hit until "Turn Off the Lights."

18

Straight *Into* Compton!!
Headed to Dooto's Music Center

Fuck the Police – My Story

While at the Eve a local sheriff sergeant got extremely pissed off at me for an answer I gave him when he asked about the availability of a female customer he was attracted to at Eve After Dark, and that's when my problems started. I never got beaten by the police but for several months, my life was a legal hell. It didn't help that I had been caught with guns more than once. And my neighborhood was known for selling dope.

I lived in the same neighborhood as Eve After Dark. The cop that patrolled the Eve on Friday and Saturday also patrolled my neighborhood Monday through Friday, so he knew where I lived. He would harass me just like he did the dope dealers, only in different ways. I would get tickets for backing out of my driveway, putting my car in park too close my gate. They told me I was blocking the street. I would back out of my driveway or pull up in my driveway, pull up on the side of my house to go in my yard, and they'd give me a ticket for parking too close to my driveway. They see me outside drinking a soda, they give me a ticket for loitering in front of my own damn house.

I was getting petty cases left and right. It was so bad that even after we filed a complaint on him, he just had his deputies start writing the tickets. It was so clear that was a personal issue one deputy at the risk of losing his job refused his supervisors orders to write me a ticket. He and the sergeant began to argue.

> *"Why do you keep fucking with this guy? He hasn't done shit."*

> *"If you don't write the ticket, I'm reporting you to the captain."*

> *"Let's go see the Captain. This is bullshit!"*

That night I didn't get a ticket, but the damage was already done. My problems started to spill over into Jefty's business, and that's when it became a problem for everybody. One day the old man called me into the office for the talk.

> "I think it might be best that we shut the Eve down."

It was 1985. We had a record out, but I was faced with the new dilemma of shutting down the Eve right before the peak season—Thanksgiving, Christmas, and New Year's Eve. Like a good soldier, I did it, but I also had a game plan because my daddy always told me keep a game plan. It's always good to have a good plan, but keep a backup plan.

My backup plan was right around the corner on 135th and Central in Compton. It was Dooto's Music Center, a much larger venue than the Eve, and it was in Compton where the sheriff couldn't get to me and the Compton police department was riddled with family and school buddies.

So I went to the Compton swap meet and talked to my cousin Phillip who was on the Compton P.D. He ran the security team at the swap meet. He said he would put together a security crew for me.

My security team consisted of Phillip, Reggie Wright Sr., Houie Taylor, Al Preston, and a cool but crazy Lt. Dallas Elvis (R.I.P.). With security in place, I made my proposal to Mr. Williams for every Friday night at Dooto's. He loved it.

So we shut down the Eve and I moved around the corner to Dooto's. I started promoting Dooto's on Friday nights with great success.

Shortly after that, Skateland opened right next door. The owner saw what I was doing on Fridays and offered me Saturdays at Skateland. So I'm promoting two venues on the same street, next door to each other, back-to-back. As a promoter, I was *the shit*.

When I moved my parties around the corner to Dooto's Music Center, everything changed. Now I'm under the jurisdiction of the Compton Police Department who also were my security. It was beautiful.

But! My nightmare still didn't go away because the cop still harassed me. I still lived in a dope-infested neighborhood. I was a well-dressed young Black man with a new car, and had my own business and a house in a dope-infested neighborhood. It was impossible for him not to think that and my dope-dealing homies and I were not connected. It was true that we all grew up together, played basketball together, played football together, even screwed some of the same girls, but I respected their game and they respected mine. We never crossed paths. The cops still don't understand that today.

19

Killing the Game

KDAY

We loved KDAY and KDAY loved us. KDAY was the hottest radio station in the city and they played all our records. They helped launch the careers of all the west coast acts.

Shortly after Jefty asked me to close down the Eve, right before we moved to Dooto's, my sales rep at KDAY (Rochelle Lucas) told me I might want to meet the new DJ, soon to be program director, Greg Mack. Greg and I hooked up and went to lunch.

At our first meeting, Greg's got a big old yellow Cadillac. He's from Texas. Greg's not very tall and had on cowboy boots. The first thing that came to my crazy-ass mind is the cartoon character Yosemite Sam. Greg and I hit it off immediately. He didn't understand what I had been doing, so he wanted to check it out for himself. Shortly after I opened up Dooto's, Greg came down and saw what was happening and immediately got involved. It enhanced our relationship with KDAY even more.

Greg Mack had an idea for a fifteen-minute mix for KDAY's Traffic Jam. There was no money in the budget to pay us, but they agreed to give us commercials to advertise Dooto's. I didn't trip off the money, because a true hustler finds a way to convert energy to money, and that's exactly what I did.

I asked Greg to give us a commercial spot before and after the fifteen-minute Traffic Jam—a ten to fifteen-second spot would be feasible. All they had to say was, "This Traffic Jam is brought to you by the World Class Wreckin' Cru. They are live every Friday at Dooto's Music Center located at 135th and Central." He agreed.

Greg would give us old used tape from the station. Dre and Yella would do the mixing in the four-track studio that I built. I would shoot it down to the station daily, and then I would turn around and make the Traffic Jam a twelve-inch bootleg mix and sell it.

We were pimping and counter-pimping to get our money. Think about it...I didn't have to pay for advertising, and

Dooto's was off the chain every Friday night—a lot of extra exposure.

While we were at Dooto's, Greg brought us all the hottest acts of that time, such as LL Cool J, Soul Sonic Force, Klymaxx, and some little kids who were hot as fish grease—New Edition—that took Dooto's to a whole new level. Greg and I made a lot of money together. We talk about this all the time.

Because of my work relationship with Greg and KDAY, anybody from my side of town that wanted to get anything done with KDAY always came to me first, including Eazy E. He would bug me to no end to get records to Greg, and Greg would reject them because of some of the lyrics. Eventually, it got worked out, and the rest is history.

20

Launching the Wreckin' Cru

Fremont High School was the first gig Wreckin' Cru performed. We opened for New Edition, which was sponsored by KDAY. On top of that, we performed with New Edition's after party at Dooto's.

Wreckin' Cru was killing the game on both sides of the spectrum. There was nobody else out there at the time that was more consistent than we were.

As program director, Greg Mack came up with a great concept—bringing Dooto's acts like Klymaxx, LL Cool J, and basically any artist that was hot and was about to release their record. Everything was great until we both started doing too much. We all started spreading ourselves too thin. Greg was bringing groups to Dooto's on Friday nights and to the skating rink in the Valley on Saturday nights. Wreckin' Cru started getting so big that we were hardly at Dooto's like we once were because we were usually leaving town. We were getting calls to go out of town a lot more, so the whole Dooto's thing started to dissolve—we kinda outgrew it. Shortly after that, Old Man Dootsie died and the building was sold.

Mr. Williams offered to sell me Dooto's for $200,000, and the crazy part was collectively the Cru had enough for a solid down payment. We were negotiating our CBS record deal for $100,000. I was about to buy Johnny Otis's house with a studio in it, but I was willing to pass on the house and live in Dooto's. (Dooto's was not only an auditorium. It had offices, a ticket booth, *and* a two-bedroom apartment and single apartment that were used to house acts, and also were used as dressing rooms.) Unfortunately, as usual, I couldn't get the Cru to see the vision. Not buying Dooto's was one of my few regrets.

Part IV

The Record Biz
Back in the Day

"More robberies are committed
with a pen and ink
than ever with a gun and gunpowder."
— Lonzo

21

The Feud that
Fueled the West

Let me back up and explain how I met Rodger Clayton. One night I was DJ'ing a party for these guys out in Long Beach called IP, International Promoters, and I was *doing* it! I was the DJ, light man, special effects, emcee—all this at one time. I was working the gig by myself this particular night because my roadie had to go to school and he couldn't hang out with me.

Along with being tired, I was also nervous that somebody was gonna steal all my rented equipment. I could hear my dad's words, *"Why borrow...if you borrow it and something happens to it, you gotta pay for it and you still don't have it."* But that was part of my "fake it 'til you make it" campaign.

After a while, I looked around and saw these two dudes checking out my shit. They were two guys I had seen around, but I really didn't know them. They began asking me all kinds of questions about my equipment. How much did it cost? Where did I get it from? Was it heavy? Where did I live? So while I'm trying to rock a party of 300 people and working lights, I was being interviewed by the future competition. I thought to myself, *either these muthafuckas are writing a book, or I'm gonna get robbed!*

Before long, they started going through my records, casually at first, so I didn't trip on them. Plus, sometimes people would go through my crate and then request a song. But I began to notice that the more I didn't trip, the busier these two cats got. They started pumping my rented smoke machine and turning my rented lights on and off, which at first made me very uncomfortable, but it also gave me a chance to choose my records more carefully, because as a good DJ, you have to stay in tune with your crowd or you can lose them real quick.

I kept my eyes on these muthafuckas just in case they tried the old snatch and run, but come to find out they were just two equipment-challenged brothers who had the desire to be DJs but didn't know a mirror ball (disco ball) from a basketball. They introduced themselves as Andre (who later became The Unknown DJ) and Rodger (a.k.a. The Ace of Dreams, later to be known as Mr. Prince of Uncle Jamm's Army).

Seems Rodger and some fellow promoters had been checking me out from to time to time and thought I could use some help. Rodger and I stayed in contact. We all became buddies, and later Andre joined my Crew. Shortly after that, I got Rodger a job at Record Shack—a place that changed both of our lives.

Rodger and I were always finding ways to one-up each other. He would find out what I was doing and take advantage of it. And I'd do the same to him. When I would bring an act in—Kurtis Blow and Run DMC—he didn't want to pay for plane tickets, he just piggybacked off of my shit. It was more fuel on the feud. He wouldn't even offer to pay half. I'm like, *how in the hell I'ma buy you a plane ticket but you muthafuckas are at Rodger's doin' the same show y'all did at my club?*

Usually what promoters would do: I'd go get the act Friday, the other guy would take him Saturday. I'd pay for him to get here, the other guy would pay for him to go home. That was usually the deal. But Rodger never did that. It made for an awkward situation for me, so after that, I stopped booking acts that way.

Uncle Jamm's Army vs Disco Construction

My thing was consistency and frequency; Rodger's thing was size. He did parties at the Biltmore Hotel, Queen Mary, and some at the Convention Center. I did these same

121

hotels while owning Eve After Dark, and would double my money by having the after party at the Eve.

Rodger was known to be the ultimate hater. Dave Chappelle does this skit about the Haters Club—it's funny as hell. Buck Nasty doesn't like kids. He took kids' money; he was the worst hater of all time. Rodger was the original Buck Nasty. His nickname was Rodger "Hatin' Clayton." He had an overbearing attitude, that real deep voice, and he was always quick to tell somebody *"fuck you!"* He would go on like he was big and bad, talking shit until you called his bluff. Then he'd calm down and talk like he had some sense. When it came to records, venues and acts, he was a megalomaniac—that shit was crazy.

I didn't realize how much impact Rodger and I had on the west coast until one day they called us all together for a photograph of all the west coast players "A Day in The West". They had done it in New York—all the hip hop players of New York—*everybody* from Cool Herc down to whoever was the latest guys, and they're sitting on the steps of a building somewhere back east. It was like the Class of '80-something or 90-something, whatever it was. They wanted to do the same thing here in L.A.

It took about a year to get everybody notified that on this particular day, we're taking a picture with all the hip hop players on the west coast. Just about everybody showed up. It was downtown. It looked like it was an old football field or something, I'm not sure, and it had bleachers. We all stood up on these bleachers.

On this particular day late in the 90's, Rodger and I were pretty cool. We were taking pictures with different people, everybody giving pats on the back, collectively and individually.

Rodger, Big Boy and Lonzo
at the shoot for "A Day in the West"

So it came time to take the picture, and this was the first time we had ever gotten any mass recognition from our fellow west coast homies. Rodger and I were sitting up top talking shit. We didn't feel like we deserved anything special, we were just doing what we do. On this day, we were just getting along. All of a sudden we hear somebody's voice...

"Where's Lonzo and Rodger at?"

Somebody said, "There they are, up there!"

"Tell them two muthafuckas to come down here, 'cause if it wasn't for them, wouldn't none of us be down here!"

So we start making our way down from the top to the bottom, and everybody stood up and gave us a round of applause! *Everybody* gave us a standing ovation! I don't know about Rodger, but I had to hold back the tears. I had never been recognized by my homies, and very few times do you get that kind of love while you're alive. As we walked down, we got pats on the back, and somebody shouted out...

"Better hurry up 'fore they start fightin'!"

22

Macola Records
and Don MacMillan

Before Macola Records opened up, Don MacMillan was a foreman for a big pressing plant—I believe it was Cadet Records. Cadet Records was a blues label that had all the blues guys back in the day. They went out of business and Don bought all their equipment and moved to Hollywood.

Basically, Don was just pressing records until a local record man by the name of Duffy Hooks got with him and introduced him to various independent record distributors. The independent record distributors would buy from Don and sell records all over the country.

Well, Don knew manufacturing. Duffy knew distribution; he was a record man. And somehow or other, Don and

Duffy were able to put together a distribution situation that allowed Don to press records—not free, but at a very low cost for up-and-coming record labels, which gave him the edge on anybody that wanted to release a record.

To make a record back in the day, after you recorded it, just to do the manufacturing "parts" (the printing, labels, mastering) to make a record might cost you about six or seven hundred dollars. So Don would sometimes front those costs for independent artists to help them get out, but he would also sell records and if the record sold well, the plan was he would deduct his costs from the sale of the record and pay you the balance.

Macola Records was the best *and* worst thing that happened to the new artist. Macola was like our main outlet for products. Their slogan should have been: *you bring it, we press it, and we're not paying you shit.* That's how Don MacMillan did his business. Unlike most artists, because of my record distribution experience, I had accounts locally and nationally that bought our records, allowing us to keep a positive cash flow.

We would take Don a tape. He would do the plating process and label it. In a few days, you were able to go pick up some records. The problem with Don was that he was selling more records out the back door than we were selling out the front door. This dude was doing so much shit behind our backs with our products that some artists

126

were still finding out about it in the year 2013, and might still be finding out to this day!

Macola had all the hottest artists of that time coming through his company. There was Egyptian Lover, L.A. Dream Team, World Class Wreckin' Cru, Timex Social Club, JJ Fad, Unknown DJ, Arabian Prince, Bobby Jimmy and the Critters, and Easy E and N.W.A. Don was so powerful, he could've been the fifth major record distributor in the country, but instead he settled for the minor league training ground—that's my personal opinion. Because he didn't want to pay his clients, everybody eventually moved on.

During our time at Macola, we were performing at Dooto's Music Center in Compton. We were hot shit, and we had Greg Mack on the radio making it happen. One thing you gotta understand is that with Macola and Greg Mack in the mix and me running Dooto's, we had a trifecta going and that would be hard for anyone else to duplicate without being a major artist. What I mean by that is we had airplay, distribution, and live performance. That is very hard to do today unless you are a major name artist.

Sometimes we would leave the studio with a cassette tape, give it to Greg Mack, and sometimes before we got on the 110 freeway headed home, we would hear our record being played! This definitely gave us more recognition, to the point that Macola had orders, I had orders…we had backorders up to four to five hundred units in Los Angeles alone because of the airplay.

Hip hop and rap records were very rare back then, especially on the west coast. So anything that came out was damn near a guaranteed hit for us. We also had a weekly party that we would do at Dooto's that was off the chain. KDAY's first mix masters came out of World Class Wreckin' Cru. I know many may think Julio G and Tony G were the first. They were mix masters, but the *original* mix masters were Dre and Yella for KDAY.

But! Don was a thief, first and foremost. So he would get the record out and sell it to his people and he wouldn't report to anybody. Nobody knew what Don was doing. Nobody ***ever*** knew what Don was doing. When I outgrew my original record manufacturer for World Class Wreckin' Cru (Bill Smith Custom Records in El Segundo), I went to Don. Don gave me, like everybody else, a one-sheet record deal to do the distribution; he wanted fifteen percent and all we had to do was deliver the masters and he would take care of everything and deduct it from the sales.

Well, little did we know that by delivering the masters to Don, we pretty much gave him...not the legal right, but in his own mind, rights to sell your record worldwide and give you little to none of the money. Basically, Don was providing product to record distributors and we had no idea who they were selling to. When Wreckin' Cru was doing shows at Dooto's, all of a sudden I started getting phone calls to go do gigs in Louisiana, Mississippi, Texas, and I'm like, *how the hell did you hear about us? The record's out here; I never shipped the record nowhere!* By now, Don's shipping records all over the country and people started becoming aware of our music and they wanted us to perform.

So Don, through his ability to press records and distribute records to independent record distributors, made himself the man to go to in the 80's. If you could get out of a studio with your tape, Don could get your stuff to the marketplace. Now, the next problem was getting paid.

Don distributed the records for ninety-nine percent of the artists that came out on the west coast at some point in time. He had the Who's Who of west coast rap. Eazy E and N.W.A.—their first project came through Macola.

Unfortunately, Don's business model (fronting all the money for doing the pressing and whatever the case may be), didn't work out that well because he had no quality control. Don would press anything. He would throw it against the wall and if it stuck, he'd keep on pressing it. If you brought a record with two crickets fucking, Don would press it. And at some point in time, he started having more returns than he had sales, and then all the artists started leaving Don, going on to get major record deals.

World Class Wreckin' Cru, my group, was one of the first ones to leave to get a major record deal. After we left, Don's flow of traffic stopped coming through because he was no longer the go-to guy. There were other options by this time.

Along with being one of the first groups to leave, we were also one of the first groups to go back to Don, because World Class Wreckin' Cru and Stereo Crew got dropped a year after we signed with CBS. When we returned to Macola Records, we were met with a substantial number of returns—and his new business partners, some serious folks from the east coast. At some point in time, Don had decided to take on some partners, a group of very serious cats from back East. They brought in some new money that Don was hoping would stop the exodus of acts going to major labels. But it didn't work.

23

New York Partners

When we went back to Macola, Don had this new partnership with some gentleman from back East. I'm sitting in the office with Don and his new partners, and I told them in front of Don that he was gonna steal. And they told me in front of Don, with a straight face, looking Don right in the eyes, "If we catch Don stealing, we're gonna take Don out to the pressing plant, put a funnel up his ass and pour vinyl up his ass 'til it comes out his eyeballs."

I want to emphasize that this guy was not playing. He was very serious. I'm sitting right there listening. Don's sitting there smoking cigarettes. He tried to play it off like it was a joke, but this cat wasn't joking.

Now, when these guys came to town, I was informed by a very reliable source to have minimum private contact with them because some of their business practices might be very detrimental to my health. Some former business associates had been blown up in cars, had been shot…basically, I'm in bed with the Sopranos!

These cats were from back east—I ain't calling no names, I ain't that stupid—but I will tell you they gave me a contract. They wanted a piece of my 12-inch **Turn Off the Lights,** and they wanted a piece of the album. They gave me a check for $25,000 to do the album and a contract that was forty pages long with amendments that went through the alphabet three and a half times. This was the most confining contract known to man. They wanted a piece of every dime I ever made again in life. If I got a job at McDonald's, they wanted to get paid. They tried to corner every way to get paid that they possibly could.

My manager at the time was a very nice lady loosely related to some of these guys from New Jersey. She knew these guys pretty well.

"Hey, don't worry about it," she told me, "I'ma renegotiate the contract."

"What do I do with the $25 G's?"

"Cash the check, bring me my cut, and I'll deal with it."

So I left it in her hands. Shortly after that, I got a phone call from Priority Records.

"Hey man, we want a license to Turn Off the Lights for a compilation album, which is very common; we do it on a regular basis. We're gonna give you $4,000 to license this song on a compilation album, and if we do this, you'll get a royalty."

No problem. So I called my manager to make sure we were okay. She says no problem. The contract hasn't been done yet. It's still technically my record; I can do a licensing deal. I wouldn't sell it, but I could license it to them with no problem.

So I did the deal. And after I did the deal, only a couple of weeks had passed when I got a phone call from a very irate individual wanting to kick my ass.

"What did I do?"

"God dammit, you sold my record to somebody else and I'm gonna blah blah blah…"

"Man, I didn't sell nothing! I just did a licensing deal."

Okay. Well, this heated individual and I went to Priority Records and met with the president. He threatened to kick the president's ass. The president's sitting there with a bottle of Jack Daniels on the table, shaking, pouring shots of Jack Daniels while we're having this meeting, and while we're sitting there he ordered another check for $4,000 for *these* guys. I'm witnessing the whole thing.

When we left Priority Records, although he was originally pissed at me, when we got outside the elevator, he was happy. He was cool. He was all jovial.

Next, I get a phone call from back east! It's six o'clock a.m. L.A. time, and I get a phone call that wakes me up. It's a guy with a real raspy voice asking for Alonzo Williams. I identified myself, and he proceeded to identify himself.

"This is so-and-so from back east. I understand we have a problem."

"What problem do we have, sir?"

I've always maintained my respectfulness on all phone calls, especially if I don't know you.

"What's the problem, sir?"

"Well, we did a deal for your record and I understand you did a deal someplace else! And if you were here on the east coast, guys like you would be in the Hudson River."

WHAT? Now I'm wide awake.

"Excuse me, what do you mean?"

So he tells me how they gave me a contract and I voided the contract... I haven't voided anything!

"The contract is still in negotiation," I respond. "Bottom line is, the product is still mine. I only did a licensing deal...we still can do our deal, that's not a problem here. It's just that we gotta get a contract we both can live with."

So after about a fifteen to twenty-minute conversation, he was no longer threatening. In fact, he was kinda understanding, but from that point on, every time I went to Macola, I carried my pistol.

Shortly after that, while I'm carrying a pistol to Macola, I was also being reminded not to get in the car with certain individuals because upset associates had been known to set car bombs. And this mofo wants to take me to lunch every day and drive his car. I had more excuses not to do lunch than mofos in handcuffs trying not to go to jail. Aw, this shit was crazy! I realize I don't wanna live like this anymore. I don't wanna do this. I don't want to have to carry a gun—my daddy used to say, "I'd rather be judged by twelve than carried by six."

I'm not a gangster! But I ain't nobody's punk either. All the while I'm experiencing this first-hand, I'm watching my former label mates tell the world about all the gangsta shit they're supposed to have done, and I'm laughing my ass off.

24

The Macola Implosion

The mob didn't come demanding their cut of everything because the shit got so crazy with Macola. When Macola was being run, I don't know whether they got to Macola as an investment or something shady. I remember seeing multiple FedEx boxes, the big thick ones, being busted open by the secretary and money falling out of 'em. We're talking about possibly hundreds of thousands of dollars over a period of time, so my little $25,000 wasn't any money.

All of a sudden word got out that Macola had these shady partners. People were already reluctant to do business with Don. Now nobody wanted to be bothered with him. At least when Don stole from you, you could go back in the back and take your own shit back and sell it—not with these new partners watching Don and everybody else, making sure nobody stole from them. Nobody wanted to be bothered with him, so the whole thing kinda imploded.

Once it imploded, it was just like watching Goodfellas! Once they got everything they wanted out of Don, once they got him in debt, everything got sold off. The pressing plants, all the parts and whatever—*everything* got sold off. They may have gotten their money from the liquidation.

For the most part, as far as Don being the record man, he no longer had that power. Plus, CDs started coming into play. Records no longer were the big deal. CDs were kicking records in the butt. Cassettes were also a part of the record era, but that threat wasn't as big as CDs became. So as CDs became more prevalent in the music industry, Don's ability to even *sell* records started to diminish. So as the east coast partners saw the handwriting on the wall, they stepped away from Don.

When they stepped away from Don, they just pretty much left everybody alone. I think my "Turn off the lights in the Fast Lane" album was probably one of the only projects still at Macola. Don went into bankruptcy owing me close to $400,000—I'm quite sure the partners got a good chunk of that. That's why I didn't get paid. That hurt to no end. It was really a hell of a time.

Don could have been the fifth major record distributor in the country, but he was too greedy. It's common knowledge that Don was not a naturalized citizen. He was from Norway. His wife worked for the Norwegian cruise lines. When I and many other people tried to sue Don, there was nothing left to get. We knew Don had stolen hundreds of thousands, if not millions, of dollars from record artists over a period of about eight or nine years. My suspicion was that his wife took the money in a trunk to Norway and the money was never seen again. Whether I'm right or wrong, we'll never know.

As crazy as what I'm about to say is gonna sound, being in direct contradiction to what I've said previously, Don still was the best thing that ever happened to the west coast hip hop scene. He allowed us to make records when nobody else would. He allowed us to press records when we didn't have money.

I know this sounds totally insane for me to say right now, but without Don there would have been no west coast hip hop scene. He showed most of us how to make and distribute records—at a very expensive cost, but at that time there was no school, class (at college or online), or seminar to take to learn "Record Business 101." We got our education from Don MacMillan and Macola Records' school/university of hard knocks. All I can say is *that was an expensive education.*

25

What I Had to Deal With

My crew did not have the business knowledge to understand the difference between recoupment money and royalty money. They did not take into account that I actually saved some of mine where they spent all of theirs. They did not allow for the fact that I had a $40,000 line of credit from my first house that was already fully paid for. It didn't look good to them that I could afford to get a new house. They felt I was somehow cheating them of some money. They forgot I was already "nigga-rich" from the success of the club and various promotions I had done before and while the Cru was together.

My old house and car were already paid for long before I signed the deal with CBS, but after we got the deal, I figured now would be a great time to upgrade. So I purchased the new house with a studio in it and purchased a nicer car. Don't get me wrong, I had utilized my funds, too, but I did it in on a higher level. But purchasing these things made me look a little suspect in their eyes. Not to mention the "Shirley effect" was still hanging over my head—her telling them that I had stolen a bunch of money from them. Shirley was our first manager. The guys were still suspicious based on some misinformation they had heard from her.

Now we had signed with Jerry Heller as our manager. Time dragged on and CBS was really not gigging us and didn't release our album very fast because of the various heavyweight artists on the CBS roster, including Luther Vandross' release and Teena Marie's release, etc. Our executive producer, Larkin Arnold, had left CBS, so now we had nobody in the company fighting for us. We pretty much were just languishing on the shelf at that time, losing momentum for doing our gigs, so now things were changing considerably. We spent an entire summer basically doing nothing.

We did manage to go to England for a couple of days, playing the Fresh Fest at Wembley Stadium. That was an adventure within itself, but basically our gigs kind of dried up for quite some time. The Fresh Fest helped lift the Cru's morale because our money well was pretty much dry.

I was on the verge of a new generation of recording artists to go with the brand new studio that I had. I got all the local producers and rappers to come out to the studio. It was making a cool profit for a while.

We were on the shelf at CBS for six months. They finally released our album, Rapped in Romance, with little to no promotion due to a major independent promoter scandal that had everybody shaking in their boots. Shortly after that, they dropped us and Ice Cubes group Stereo Crew. Both groups went into the Studio. Stereo Crew changed their name to CIA (Cru' In Action). They made a three-song EP that was a strong Beastie Boy-ish sound. Wreckin' Cru went into the studio and cut an EP titled "Housecalls," another song about Dre. We returned to Macola for distribution, only to find out Don McMillan was pissed at us for initially leaving. As the first ones to leave Macola, we had kind of spearheaded an exodus out of Macola—L.A. Dream Team, Egyptian Lover, Club Nouveau, and more.

Don had recalled every record we ever made prior to our return—Surgery, Juice, the album, cassette, everything. Had them in his warehouse and used those returned records and their manufacturing costs as justification for not paying Kru-Cut for their current releases.

Although the two records sold moderately well, there was never a check issued for royalties *or* recoupment. Macola was claiming Kru-Cut owed it $50,000 in manufacturing costs for previous product. Now I got CIA—Ice Cube,

Jinx, and K-Dee—looking at me crazy, asking questions, along with Dre, Yella, and Shakespeare. Nobody was trying to hear what the situation consisted of. All they knew was they didn't get any money.

I was thinking of a plan that could save Kru-Cut and help us get back on top, and that plan was to make a new record. The guys didn't want to, because they felt like they didn't get paid for the last one. So I was trying to explain to them that if we cut a new record, by the time it came out, we'd be in the black with Macola and we could start getting checks again. For some reason they still didn't understand how the music industry worked. They didn't want to budge.

Because we were already in debt, I felt the best way for us to get out of debt was to go to the format of a slow song like Lovers which had gotten us so much notoriety and gigs. *Nobody* was feeling me. I had to bet on myself, and I thought that a new slow song was the best move. So that's when I decided to record "Turn Off the Lights." The rest of the guys were so adamant about not wanting to do it, they refused to write their own parts.

One day I'm out in the streets slinging records at the Compton Swap Meet where I go see Mr. Park to sell records, and I remember something this girl told me about a week before that...

"If you don't do this right, don't turn off the goddamn lights! If you ain't gonna do this right, don't turn 'em off, 'cause I don't play! If you're going to do it to me, you better do it well, 'cause I'm a helluva woman and for me it takes a helluva man!"

Have you ever been sick and you just start vomiting and you couldn't stop? That's how the lyrics to Turn Off the Lights came to me. It was like I got ill for a minute. I had to stop what I was doing, and I wrote the whole damn thing down. The whole song came to me—everybody's part—everything came to me while I was sitting in the parking lot at the Compton Swap Meet!

I put it together and made it happen. I couldn't convince the fellas to go to the studio to do the shit without a monetary incentive. Nobody wanted to do this. ***Nobody***. Not Dre, Yella, none of them.

"Man, fuck that shit! We need to start doing some more hip hop! Hip hop! More hip hop!"

I tried to reason with them.

"That ain't what we *do*! We don't do hip hop! We do dance rap! You can call it hip hop if you want to, but we do dance rap. And our biggest, strongest song is Lovers!"

"Fuck that! We ain't doin' shit!"

They were doing a temper tantrum on my ass! Now my money is limited and they're giving me an ultimatum.

"If you don't give us some money, we ain't doin' shit."

Dre had this beat he had been playing with, so I ran the words past him. He liked the song, but he still didn't wanna do it.

Eventually I was able to get all of them some money to come and record the track. I had all their parts already written out, so they just had to read the parts. I'm proud to say, Turn Off the Lights was totally written by me. This song was our farewell song. They knew once November arrived, they would be free artists to do whatever they wanted to do.

When we made Turn Off the Lights, none of them had any money, as usual. I made Turn Off the Lights with my last four grand. I bet my house note, my light bill and my car note to make that song. I stepped out on faith and faith only.

Blind Leading the Blind

Handling our business back in those early days, we thought we were doing shit right. I hear so much about how the

144

Cru got cheated, how I took advantage... They didn't understand—I didn't know shit either! Yes I was the boss, but the record game was totally new to me and no one was offering any record business lessons. All I knew was I'd get a check from Macola, take out what I was owed for manufacturing and labeling, and cut the royalties with the guys.

No accounting system was available to us to account for royalties back then. I didn't see the first royalty system come out 'til about 1990; it cost $1,500. Macola didn't give us any accounting—just gave me a check and I cut it up.

My Wreckin' Cru guys were money predators. They went through money like a crackhead in a dope house, and I was the supplier. At one point in time, the money dried up. That was the beginning of our fallout. They gave me the ultimatum and I took my last four grand and made Turn Off the Lights.

I did what was best for everybody. They did what was best for *them*. Later, they had the nerve to say that I knew the song was gonna be a hit and that's why I didn't wanna renew their contracts! I heard this shit second-hand from a close reliable source, because we had stopped talking face to face. That was the craziest shit I had ever heard come out of somebody's mouth in my life. I may be a bad muthafucka in somebody's eyes, but I ain't no genie. I cannot predict the future, although I always think positive about anything I do. I had no idea Turn Off the Lights would be as successful as it was, but I thank God that it was.

26

The Cru
Turning Off the Lights

After Macola gave me my initial recording investment back, I was told that Jerry gave the fellas the impression it was a lot more money than it actually was. I can't really say for sure that it was Jerry, but as far as I knew, he was the only one who knew I had been paid anything.

That's when everything fell apart. That was my second time being caught up in a financial scandal on some bullshit. The fellas felt like they should get paid also, but that was the first check that I'd received from Macola in a long time, and it was only reimbursement for my recording expenses. For my Cru not being businessmen—just basically a bunch of youngsters—that was like the straw that broke the camel's back, although it wasn't even a toothpick.

Once again, I had to explain to the fellas that this check was me getting my investment back; it had nothing to do with profit for the Wreckin' Cru. But they didn't understand basic business. Shirley's lies, my new house and car—in their minds, it all added up to me doing something shady. There was also the fact that Eazy was telling them all the things that they could do if they went with him. It became hard for me to defend myself, although I didn't feel like I should have had to. In the end, we parted ways. They were basically like *fuck you and have a nice life*, and I was like *same here*.

Shakespeare Remembers...

"The whole meltdown came like this. Timex Social Club was on Macola Records. The lead singer had fell out with the group and he wanted to bounce. Matter of fact, he had fell out with Jay King. He wanted to bounce and he wanted his royalties, and it was an issue where they weren't givin' him his royalties, so he went and got a lawyer and initiated a lawsuit. And because he initiated the lawsuit, nobody from Macola could get paid for no record until they resolved this issue with Timex Social club.

148

"Somebody said that Alonzo had gotten all this money for Turn Off the Lights and wasn't givin' the guys nothin'. We had a meeting at Lonzo's house and Lonzo was defending himself and finally just asked the guys what they wanted to do, keep on bein' a group or what... Eazy E was in Dre's ear. He had had all this drug money, so he convinced Dre, 'Listen man, if you come with me, your troubles will be over.' So at that point, Dre decided he was done with Wreckin' Cru. Then of course, when Dre was done, Antoine was the follower and he followed Dre. That left me and Lonzo, and we couldn't do it with just the two of us, so things just kinda devolved from there..."

As a group, we had come extremely far, but the minute adversity set in, my original members were ready to jump ship and move on to something else. Unfortunately, they became influenced by the words of others and they were too blind to see that the same person that was in their ear was the same person that wanted to sabotage their success.

Although I consider Jerry a buddy, I also think he kind of played favorites. Jerry knew he could influence Eric if he gave him some power. He's a businessman, and I find that people tend to gravitate toward those they can influence a lot easier. These guys never asked questions. Whatever Jerry said, they had no business knowledge to ask questions. They had no basic business knowledge to

149

understand what was involved when asked for certain things.

The Game of Divide and Get Paid

So Dre and Yella left the Wreckin' Cru. I see this a lot in groups. You can rest assured, whoever the public likes the most will always become a solo artist. If there is a person in a group, like Beyoncé in Destiny's Child, R. Kelly with Public Announcement, Michael Jackson of the Jackson 5... I mean it's been happening for decades. It's how the music business goes.

When you have a group, you have four or five individuals but one manager and one lawyer for the group. Now sometimes, the group members may have their own individual lawyers based on the type of negotiations they're doing, but for the most part, it's usually one person that handles the whole thing. But when you can split that group up, now you have one manager for the group and one manager for this person, and depending on the relationship, you can influence that.

If you've ever seen the story of the Temptations, David Ruffin's so-called manager got between him and the Temptations and had him thinking he was God's gift to music! He was a bad boy, but he was a Temptation! It was never supposed to be David Ruffin and the Temptations! People do that to manipulate you, because now your ego kicks in and you wanna feed that monster! And when that monster gets hungry, sometimes in order to feed itself, it will eat its own friends.

27

Big Hit, No Band

From the time Turn Off the Lights was cut all the way 'til January, I was down to my last money. I was betting on that single, hoping it would save my ass. Macola sent a few records up to this record promoter in Frisco to get the song on KSOL and again, nothing happened until January 1987.

All of a sudden I look up and I'm in the Top 10 single list for Turn Off the Lights. Turn Off the Lights is doing well! The craziest part of this is, I no longer have a group to perform with, nor any money to tease them with about coming on the road.

Turn Off the Lights really elevated my reputation. Apparently, the radio stations didn't realize we were no longer with CBS, and they treated Turn Off the Lights like it was on a major label. The fact that it was a great record helped get it played on stations the original Cru had never been played on before. The phone was ringing off the hook for gigs, but I had no group to perform with.

By this time, the Cru had stopped coming around to the house. We had little to no communication, and the only communication tie we had was Jerry. Turn Off the Lights became so popular, Jerry was getting calls for gigs; the only problem for me was I'd be performing with Eazy E, Ice T, Just Ice, and N.W.A. I'm the only non-gangsta act on the bill, but I got the biggest record. Just the thought of doing this felt as awkward as hell.

I was being offered anywhere from $5,000 to $7,500 a night to perform and I'm turning them down because it just didn't feel right. After turning down about seven or eight gigs totaling between $50,000 and $70,000, Jerry got on my ass.

"What do you wanna do, feel sorry for yourself or make some money?"

I was pissed and depressed, but I decided to make some money. That's when I grabbed the Uzi Bros. I also grabbed Richie Rich, a local rapper, and Battle Cat, an up-and-coming producer, along with Mona Lisa, my original singer.

We hit the road. Now not only did I have a back-up band, but I also had some support if some shit jumped off.

I got a top 10 single on my hands; the radio didn't know that we were no longer signed to CBS. There was no e-blast or press conference to inform them that this song was released on Kru-Cut Records. Basically, they weren't knowledgeable about the change. That song was played constantly in heavy rotation.

The Uzi Bros. had my back. They were a local club band from up north. They were originally called Precision. I met them with my brother Randy, and he loved 'em. We all got along great. They were real musicians. Wil Roc, their keyboard player, had played on Turn Off the Lights. These were some no-joke old-school cats like myself, and I knew they would be great to have on the road if I had a problem.

Turn Off the Lights took off on the charts; it was in the Top 10 of most markets. It topped out at #1 in a few places with little to no promotion, just because it was a good record.

Every Man for himself

At the end of the day, this is business. It's every man for himself. I'm pissed, but I ain't mad. I trusted people who I thought were homies—friends—but again, it's every man for himself. You can't always believe what somebody tells you when they're shaking your hand or smiling at your face. You have to cover your own ass at all times. That's the nature of the entertainment business. I'm saying this not only explaining myself, but for people who will be reading this book that have aspirations of being in the entertainment business.

One thing I can honestly say about the entertainment business—it turns homies into plaintiffs and defendants. What people do one day for love and excitement...once money enters the scenario, everything changes. Especially what's perceived by small people as big money. This is how shit starts. Ain't nobody stupid at all. You're trying to give certain people the benefit of the doubt, but at some point in time, your own sanity comes into question if you don't look at certain things for what they are.

I discovered Michel'le in my backyard. Nobody wanted her on the label, nobody wanted her on the song. *I* put her out there. Turn Off the Lights became a hit record and next thing you know, she's on Ruthless Records. You got people in your camp that are working against you. This is what I've been surrounded with for most of my business career. So when certain things happen, I don't expect it, but I ain't surprised. I am not surprised.

It's imperative that I say these things. In life, people interpret the same situations differently. I can only speak for myself and what I saw.

28

Michel'le

Turn Off the Lights was written for Mona Lisa, the same girl that sang Lovers, but Mona wasn't available. So there was this young girl I had met maybe eighteen months before then, Michel'le. I had just come off the road and a guy called me up about her.

"Hey man, I got this girl I want you to hear."

At one time, everybody was bringing me somebody. Everybody with lips that was trying to rap, they brought to my house.

"My baby…"

"My son…"

"My nephew…"

"My cousin…"

"Man, I got a dog that can rap!"

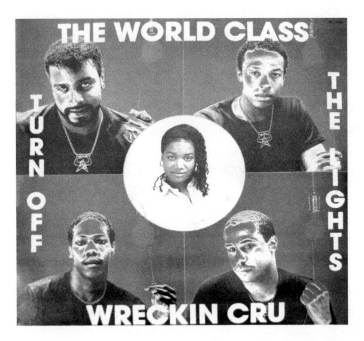

Lonzo, Dre, Shakespeare, Yella and Michel'le

I was the **man** for a while! If they had **any** type of vocal
ability, they were coming to me. I was kinda burnt out on
listening to unrecorded acts most of them had limited skills.
Most of the people who I heard were **not** all that. I had to
let this dude know I really wasn't that enthused.

"Man, I just got off the road. I got a date. I gotta GO!"

"Man please, please, please! *Please* listen to this girl!"

"Okay, you got fifteen minutes."

I take them to the house, to the studio, and she won't sing. She's bashful. She won't sing!

"Man, what is this? I got a date! I got shit to do…"

So she turns her back, and she starts singing…and she is phenomenal! While she's singing, I walk around in front of her to see if she has a recorder in her blouse and is faking it. What is she doing? But when she opened her mouth to talk, oh my *God*, she got such a squeaky-ass voice! How did this shit happen?

Time passed and I needed to get in the studio and work on this new song. The problem was, Mona was in Connecticut working with super-producer Kashif. At that time, he was a hot cat, very hot.

I wanted to get the song finished while I had Dre and them on line to do it. So I brought Michel'le back to the studio to record the female parts, but this little bashful thing was too damn shy! I was irritated. Got in the studio and she opened her mouth to speak, and everybody is looking like, "Why **her**?

After a while, we turned the lights off and she started to sing. *Now* she sang her ass off, but when it came to my signature note, the last note, she couldn't do it. And everybody in the studio—Dre and everybody else—they were *hot.*

"Man, fuck this Minnie Mouse sounding broad! Let's wait for Mona!"

"Nah, we can't wait for Mona. We gotta do this now. I got studio time, I gotta get this shit out of here."

I had to make an executive decision in order to get the job done. They didn't like her voice at all, but at end of the day it was my call. So the engineer, Donovan, told her what to do, spliced it together and made it work. That's how we got Turn Off the Lights done. After that, the shit blew up.

Michel'le was a great singer, though her voice was a different quality from Mona's. I can only imagine that her speaking voice would be hard to deal with in an intimate situation, but I guess it would be erotic to some. She came to me with no experience, and she got her first shot on a record from me.

Turn Off the Lights became a big hit. At this time, Jerry was managing World Class Wreckin' Cru *and* N.W.A. I heard that whoever had Michel'le signed had a deal waiting for him at Atlantic Records. There was no way for Eazy to know that unless Jerry told him.

I tried to sign her. She gave me every excuse in the world not to sign with Kru-Cut, then I found out she had signed a production deal with Ruthless, which later turned into a record deal with Atlantic. She and Dre had become intimate and she had signed with Ruthless Records—Eazy E's company.

Jerry knew how I operated. If there was a record deal for Michel'le for $160,000—that's what the deal was supposed to have been for—if I had her signed, nine times out of ten, I would have probably done the same thing I did before, which was to hire a lawyer, do the deal, and cut Jerry out. Not saying I'm cold-hearted chicken-shit, but it just doesn't make sense to give away $32,000 (20% of $160,000) when the deal is already done; all we gotta do is take advantage of it.

Michel'le's first album went platinum. It was a good album, but at the end of the album, one of the last things she said was, "I want to thank Lonzo, although he never paid me."

That really damaged my reputation on the streets. Why would she say that? Once again, I became the victim of someone's inexperience. That *really* pissed me off. Once again, I was fighting for my rep. Michel'le didn't take into account all the advances I had given her that needed to be recouped. She didn't take into account that, as with Mona, her singing on Turn Off the Lights was "work for hire" and she was not due any royalties. Michel'le was never signed to Kru-Cut. Mona was paid to sing on "Lovers" and she toured with us. Michel'le was paid to sing on Turn Off the Lights; there was no touring with her and there were never any royalties due to her.

Because Michel'le said that one line, I was almost knocked out of the record business. I spent four or five years defending myself from that one little line. Between Michel'le, Yella, and Dre spreading complaints despite check stubs and countless receipts and all the off-the-record times they got money from me, people kept hearing the same story. There were a few people who still trusted and loved me and were willing to work with me.

People don't understand the power of music. Music is like mini-commercials. In order for a commercial to be effective, you have to hear it repeatedly. If you play a song over and over and over, the repetition causes the message to sink into one's mind. The public constantly hearing that "Lonzo don't pay" was like a negative mini-commercial that it took me years to recover from.

Despite all the good things I've accomplished in the industry, all the successes that people have achieved coming through me, and all the millions of dollars that have been generated springing from Lonzo, I find it amazing that outsiders who misunderstand the business still focus on the few dollars they heard didn't get paid right. And the ignorant and the "nut riders" still continue to spread myth.

29

Back on the Road
with a New Cru

I went to Macola and he gave me twenty-five grand to record the album, "Turn off the Lights in the Fast Lane." The Uzi Bros. and I went to the studio…I have to say that was not the best thing to do.

I rushed into the studio musically unprepared, and it showed. For the first time ever I'm in the studio totally unprepared, no songs ready, no demos done—just me and the band in a hurry to get finished so we can hit the road.

I had to quickly transition myself from a music writer to a producer of live instruments. That alone was a totally

World Class Posse

different move for me. It's one thing to tell a programmer to give me a beat four or eight bars, sequence it and drop it in the loop. It's a whole 'nother thing to tell a talented musician, don't give me a solo—just play. That was extremely hard for me to do, and because of that, I felt like the album suffered. In spite of my inexperience, the album still did well because of Turn Off the Lights, but there were no follow-up singles.

Now I'm on tour with the Uzi Bros. I'm making five thousand to seventy-five hundred a night. However, that was the most awkward time in my life. Wreckin' Cru was headlining the show with opening acts being Eazy E and N.W.A. It was the craziest shit in music history. There I was headlining a show with a hit song on my hands. I had two new guys doing the parts of Yella and Shakespeare (Battlecat and Richie Rich), and I'm doing Dre's and my part.

Richie Rich

Richie Rich was with us for a few months. He was like the diplomat. He was around with everybody, still is. Gets along with everybody. Rapper, engineer, never been a formal member of a group to my knowledge. He was with the LA Dream Team for a while, stepped into the Wreckin' Cru for a while, but he's always been an entertainment entrepreneur like myself.

The trip about this phase of touring is Dre and Yella are on the sidelines watching us perform their parts on a song they recorded with the Wreckin' Cru—and we had never had a chance to perform "Turn Off the Lights" as a group. We're touring night after night, with Dre and Yella opening up for us with N.W.A. We were staying in the same hotels, and traveling on the same flights. That could have been a recipe for disaster, but the professional in me pulled through.

I had the Uzi Bros. with me, but they weren't exactly Dre and Yella. I was a big brother to those cats. The Uzi Bros. were my age or older, and I'm calling myself a band leader.

Honestly speaking, I didn't know how to be a fucking band leader. I never felt like I was the leader of the band. At this point, I got keyboard players, drummers and guitars. Everything was changing around me.

I was watching Eazy collect fifteen hundred to twenty five hundred a night for them. I was collecting five grand to seventy five hundred a night on the same tour. I'm watching guys that I raised up in the music industry, who hung out at my house on a regular basis. I kinda felt they might have had some animosity toward me because after they quit the group, I continued to move forward. The whole time we were on tour together, we never said anything to each other. Maybe a nod here or there, but no words were exchanged.

I remember being in the mall one day and I saw them in this sporting goods store that sold guns. They were looking at nine millimeters, shotguns and I'm not sure what else. I had to ask them...

"What tour are ya'll going on?"

"The same tour you're going on."

"Well I'm shopping for drawers going on a concert tour. You guys are acting like you are going to Vietnam!"

I was like, *what the fuck is going on?* The mindset of those guys had changed so much, to the point that I didn't know them anymore.

Battle Cat

Battle Cat and I are still cool. He's gonna get mad at me for telling this story, but he was another one of my success stories. He's produced Dogg Pound, Snoop Dogg, all kinda people. I can't tell my story without including him, because he's one of my protégés.

Battle Cat is a big-time producer now; he and Richie Rich were my Wreckin' Cru on tour! Richie Rich was a little older. Battle Cat was a kid, maybe about eighteen or nineteen years old when he started working with us. He loved eating pork—pork chops, pig feet, pig tails, pig knuckles. The Uzi Bros. were health nuts. They drank juices and water, ate no pork and very little meat, and every time they'd see Battle Cat order some pork ribs or something, they'd start the lecture.

"Boy, that pork's gonna kill you!"

The whole time we're on tour, Battle Cat's eating pig. You have to understand—you got five cats big as or bigger than me, and they're all loud, talking shit to this young kid about how pork was gonna mess his life up.

"It's gonna kill you! It's gonna plug up your arteries! It's gonna turn you into a pig! Boy, you gonna be fucked up!"

This one cat named Bob Dog—he was one of the funniest cats. He reminded you of Bobcat Goldthwaite, but he was a Black guy. He smoked cigarettes and talked shit.

"You gonna be dead eatin' this goddamn pork! That shit's gonna kill you! Watch! You watch!" he'd say as he's puffing away on his cigarette.

While we were on the road, Battle Cat being the young cat that he was, always wore tennis shoes. Something happened where he messed around and got a toe infection. It was really horrible! Bob told him that his feet were turning into hooves from eating all that pork! And we were all snickering while Bob kept laying it on him.

"Yeah, I told you! That shit's turning your feet into goddamn hooves! You gonna start oinkin' in a minute! You gonna fuck around and grow a goddamn tail! Your ears gonna get all curly and shit! You watch!"

The infection got so bad, we had to take Battle Cat to the hospital while we were on the road! He couldn't hardly walk, he couldn't hardly do the steps…he couldn't do shit! They gave him some antibiotics, and after he got back from the hospital, he came with an apology.

"Boss, I gotta apologize."

"What's wrong, Cat?

"I'm sorry, man, for eatin' all that pork. My feet's turnin' into hooves man, and I don't know what to do. I don't wanna have pig feet."

I'm trying my best not to laugh. I'm holding it in the best I can, and he's scared as a muthafucka. His sincerity with what he was saying was so fucking funny, to think his feet could actually turn into hooves. It showed me something about his inexperience with life. I had to respect his sincerity, but that shit was funny as hell.

When Battle Cat first got with me, it was his first time on the road. I never will forget, we each had our own individual hotel room, and Battle Cat was so excited to be on the road. I heard him hollering at somebody and I opened my door up, looked out to see Battle Cat walking down the hallway, and all he had on was some white BVD drawers and a beeper. I thought that was the most hilarious shit in the world.

But he got us in some serious trouble once. He was dealing with a girl from JJ Fad, and somehow or other, he and the girl had problems. It got physical, and her eye swole up to no end.

Wreckin' Cru was on our way to New York to play the Apollo, and I got a phone call from my now-manager Atron Gregory, telling me that when Battle Cat gets to New York, he's gonna have problems. JJ Fad had just been signed to Atlantic Records, and for Battle Cat and her to have this problem right before a photo shoot was a *big* problem for

168

them. When they found out what happened and what it was about, they wanted to *get* him! And we had to go to New York in two days where Atlantic's home base was.

It took a serious forty-five-minute phone call and calling in some favors to get us safe passage in New York because of what happened in L.A. It was a mess. Again, I'm talking to some *serious* people that had some *serious* intentions on doing bodily harm! *I* didn't do shit, but nine times out of ten, when shit jumps off, they're gonna miss somebody and hit *my* ass! Fuck that!

All the while, my former label mates are reporting gangsta shit live from the hood.

30

West Coast
Record Distributors

After about a year or so of not getting paid, Macola's going through bankruptcy. Atron Gregory was introduced to me by Jerry Heller, and he became the manager for World Class Wreckin' Cru. Come to find out Atron also managed Digital Underground, which had a gentleman in the group by the name of Tupac Shakur. Atron is a real smart cat from the Bay Area, and we hit it off very well.

West Coast Record Distributors was my idea for making money after Macola imploded. Once Macola started bankruptcy proceedings, I realized we needed a new distribution outlet in town. I got on the phone and called all the distributors that Don MacMillan was selling records to, and they agreed to buy from us. And although I had some doubters and nay-sayers, even though Atron didn't really think I could pull it off, he supported me a hundred percent.

"Man, if you'll do it, I'll see what we can do…"

I talked to my buddies—Unknown DJ, Rudy Pardee from the L.A. Dream Team, Egyptian Lover—and told them what the plan was. They liked it. Atron and I drove down to NARM. NARM is the National Association for Record Merchandisers. It was held in Palm Springs. We went to all the distributors and asked if they would consider buying from a label direct. They all told us yes. Everybody told us there was no doubt in their minds whatsoever, yes.

The four of us formed a distribution company called West Coast Record Distributors. West Coast Record Distributors was the turning point—we all fired Jerry because he was working with Eazy; we started our own thing. Meanwhile, World Class Wreckin' Cru, Kru-Cut Records, Egyptian Empire Records, Unknown DJ Techno Hop records, and LA Dream Team Records were independent companies cutting their own records. We were the heavy hitters when it came to the music in L.A. Nobody was higher than us; we had been running shit at Macola, and we were on the verge of finalizing our deal for the distribution company.

The four of us were in a powerful position and had the opportunity to make a shit-load of money, but we had another problem we needed to overcome, and that was the

171

pressing problem. I got with all my buddies and we all went to Rainbow Records and sat down with Steve, Rainbow's president. He generously gave us a line of credit of $25,000 each, so collectively it was $100,000. No credit report, no Dun and Bradstreet, just based on our sales ability and our relationships with distributors and him.

The deal was cosigned by a huge local distributor in the Valley called CRD (California Record Distributors). CRD covered most of the western United States. They basically guaranteed the pressing. They would cover the pressing cost and make sure Steve got his money, and we would collect from the rest of the country direct! A fantastic deal—nobody had a problem with it. We started distributing our own records in 1989.

Do you remember Good Fred Oil? Good Fred Oil was one of the first products made in the 70's for naturals. If you had a natural in the 70's, you had to have Good Fred Oil. Fred Ellis was a local hair guy that created Good Fred Oil back in the 70's. It was basically glycerin and water and it made your natural shine, the whole nine yards. Good Fred Oil had been out of business for a while, but Fred still owned the property.

After Fred stopped making Good Fred Oil, he turned the warehouse into a barbershop. He was kind enough to let us rent the top floor for our West Coast Record Distributors operation. Fred knew all of us. He had watched us grow up forever, so he wanted to see us be successful. He gave us a good deal.

I have to say that, because I'm trying to show connections between old school entrepreneurs and young entrepreneurs. Jefty Harris, the owner of the club I run right now, gave me a shot. Dootsie Williams gave us a shot at Dooto's. Fred Ellis of Good Fred Oil gave us (West Coast Record Distributors) a shot. I'm trying to show how things kept being passed down, and somebody who made it gave somebody else a chance to make it. That's how we were taught that it should be. Unfortunately, that's not what we have today.

West Coast Record Distributors was one of the biggest things we did on the west coast. We were always changing the game. West coast hip hop innovators always changed the game. Why do I say that? Nobody would give us record deals. We had to create our own labels. We had to have our own distribution. We had to learn record production! We had to learn *everything* it took to make a record, from the first beat to how to sell it on the phone.

Guys like myself, who had sales experience, hooked up with guys like The Unknown DJ, who had studio experience; Unknown hooked up with guys like Rudy Pardee, who also had sales experience, and we created our own distribution network. And because we did all this stuff, it made us...not really superior, but more advanced.

We weren't just artists. We were never just artists. We were forced to be businessmen. Most of us became "thousandaires" very fast. And by doing that—by having our own distribution, owning our own labels, booking our own tours—it was more work, but it made us much more well-informed about the music game. So today, almost thirty years later, I still own my masters.

West Coast Record Distributors was probably one of the most innovative things I did in my life, and we grossed a million dollars the first year! That was a LOT of money back then! But money and egos do not mix. That was a bad combination, because no matter what we did, egos always superseded the money. Egos superseded the vision.

It lasted about eighteen months. Although it was the best thing we ever did, it quickly became a problem. But it also set the trend for other distribution companies to follow our footprint. We had created something nobody else had done. People tried to emulate it. They couldn't duplicate it because they didn't have the hit makers that we had running the organization.

Basically, what others would do was, a bunch of distributors would get together, sign artists, and put them out through their network. That's not what we did. We were hit makers *ourselves*. Egyptian Lover was on the label. We had JJ Fad's "Supersonic." We had Rodney O and Joe Cooley and King T. All of our acts that we distributed were already proven acts, so when we put them out, we were in the green before we even opened our doors.

The basic structure of West Coast Record Distributors was: it was owned by the four individual partners, the four individual label owners—myself, the Egyptian Lover, Rudy from L.A. Dream Team, and Unknown DJ. Because Egyptian Lover was on tour and gigging a lot at that time, his girlfriend Lisa ran the Egyptian Empire company, and also oversaw the day-to-day activities of West Coast Record Distributors. Everybody would contribute ten percent of their gross sales to the operation of running West Coast. Not a bad deal. We would give Macola fifteen percent; some of us had to give him twenty.

We had a full staff—we had record promoters, we had radio promoters, we had a couple of assistants, we had warehouse personnel...we had a real operation! At the time we first jumped off, one of our first projects was Rodney O and Joe Cooley, their first album. Then we had

JJ Fad's project with their first single, Supersonic, on Dream Team Records. So we started off on a fantastic note. We had projects by King T, DJ Quick came through there—I mean, everybody was coming through trying to get deals from us. Some of them stayed, some of them didn't.

We had great success with this thing. With the success of Rodney O and Joe Cooley's first album, the Egyptian Empire label began doing very well. Unfortunately Lisa, who was running the operations for Egyptian Empire, felt West Coast was being entirely funded by Egyptian Empire. She didn't see the big picture.

We would get checks in for twenty-five, thirty, fifty thousand dollars. Ten percent of that would go to the operations costs of West Coast Record Distributors. The overhead might have been $1,500, plus another thousand for rent. Lisa would take the money and spend it on Egyptian Empire's office or some other shit not directly related to West Coast Record Distributors. Although we were making money, she was spending money in such a frivolous way that every week we'd have to come out of our pockets to pay payroll!

Egypt was doing his thing *big*, riding on top of the world! He was the hottest thing around at the time, driving around in a Mercedes, wearing suits every day, gold, the whole nine yards. He was like Pinky from Friday's; he was *the man*. You couldn't tell him shit, but he didn't realize the business was being mishandled in a major way. He was so busy doing *him*, he couldn't see that we *all* were getting done in.

The shit is making money but it's not growing. I'm in the office on a regular basis, Rudy's in there, Unknown's in there...Egypt's not really there—he's just out doing the celebrity thing. He was so busy playing, he forgot what game he was playing.

Meanwhile, Unknown and I partnered with Charles and gave him a piece of West Coast before Charles and I released "Compton Compilation" of Kru-Cut/City Fresh Records.

It sold 80,000 copies, but due to Lisa taking advances on Egyptian Empire product that never was released, we never received a dime. This caused some *major* problems that led to us shut the business down.

The Compton Compilation got so much attention, we were called by Atlantic Records to meet with Toby Emmerich. On the way to the meeting, Charles and I made up our minds that we were gonna sell this product and get out of West Coast. We agreed that our minimum was $75,000. Our meeting lasted maybe thirty minutes. Fifteen minutes into the meeting, Toby offered us $100,000. I'm sitting there biting my bottom lip, and I can see Charles is happy as hell. We shook hands with Toby and he told us he'd call us on Monday and send over the contract. We left that meeting elated.

Monday comes. I was in the office bright and early. Charles had a dentist's appointment; he didn't show up until later on. I waited all day for the phone call from Atlantic. To my knowledge, it never came. Charles and I were confused and we tried to contact Toby with no success.

Years later, I found out that Lisa had the call routed to her and told them we were no longer interested in the deal! Needless to say, I was pissed off, although it was several years after the fact. This revelation answered some questions about how she acted toward me when she saw me one day at the cable company in line to pay her cable bill. I was happy to see her, but she reacted like she owed me money. She was very nervous in my presence. She said something about leaving her checkbook in the car, and she left in a hurry without paying her bill.

31

Pioneer in the Old West

I've never been afraid to experience change. Change doesn't scare me. I have no problem with change. I look forward to change! So when the opportunity comes around to do some shit that I haven't done before, that's fine! That's why I'm always in a leadership position, because when things pop up, I'm like the first one that says, "Let's do it!"

You gonna tell me I can't do it? Don't *tell* me I can't do it, **show** me I can't do it! Let me try first, and if I can't do it, I'll be the first one to sit my ass back down! But if I **can** do it, let's make it happen! Follow my lead!

That's where most cats come in. That's what makes me the pioneer that I am. I will take the lead; I'm not afraid to be the first one.

Like I'm not afraid to be the first one on the dance floor. Most people go to a party and nobody wants to dance 'til somebody else dances. Fuck that! I'm gonna dance. You guys can look at me if you want to. I know I'm not the best dancer in the world, but I know if I start dancing, everybody else will start dancing.

That's how I've been in business. I'm not afraid to fail. Failure is a part of success; anything worth success is preceded by failure.

One of my guys recently called me with a question.

"Man, how come every time we do something down here at the club, everybody else follows us?"

Because people just *do* that! They say that imitation is a sign of flattery—no, that means you're a noncreative muthafucka, that's what that means. The person that follows you is a noncreative imitating sonofabitch. He can't create, so he steals. That's what happens.

Most of what I get myself involved in, I usually find my way to the top of the food chain if only in a certain area. When it came around for us to start doing hip hop, I decided, well—I got a crew. The club was starting to crack. Cameo got us recognized.

We made a lot of money with the club for a long period of time; then after a while, it started to decline because we became kinda regular. People started taking us for granted. I started bringing in acts like Kurtis Blow and Run DMC. I noticed every time I did that, the attendance in the club would spike.

Kurtis Blow

After Kurtis Blow recorded his song called "The Breaks," I called Russell Simmons, his manager, booked the flight, brought him and Davey DMX, his DJ at the time, out here and booked them for two shows. Kurtis Blow's show was really kinda crazy. He already had Christmas Rappin', he had The Breaks, but the cut we loved was AJ Scratch. He initially didn't have it in his show, but we told him to put it in because it was very popular. They performed on Friday and Saturday. The first show was off the chain—did very well. The second show didn't work out that well. But they were here for an extra two days, if I'm not mistaken.

Davey DMX was a super cool dude. He taught Yella how to scratch with turntables. He took him into the DJ booth and showed him everything—how to hold the record, how to do mixing, the whole nine yards—and that was the beginning, the first time scratching had been introduced to the west coast. We had blended and mixed, but we had never scratched. Davey DMX took maybe two days with Yella teaching him how to scratch, and Yella later taught Dre.

My turntables at the time were not professional turntables. I always bought the cheapest turntables I could get. They cost me $59 a piece, and that was a lot of money. My dad bought my first pair for me. He loaned me the money, and I mounted those two turntables in the club. Now Davey DMX introduces us to Technic 1200 turntables. I had only heard of them through DJ's when I was on the phone at Record Shack. They talked about 1200s, how great they were, but I had never seen a pair up close 'til Davey DMX brought his out here. The braking system, the way they didn't slip, they just automatically started—no wow and flutter, as they called it.

Well, because of Davey DMX introducing Yella to scratching, now I'm being pressured by Yella and the rest of the guys to spend $700 on a pair of turntables—*OH MY GOD!* You're talking '82, '83! Talk about a brother that was stressing! Ain't no way in the *world* I was planning to spend $700 for some turntables! But after a little convincing and a couple of good weekends, I finally broke down and bought them, and it was the best thing I ever did for the Cru, because having the proper equipment just changed the whole sound.

There was a lot of scratching back then, and you really couldn't scratch with belt drive turntables because the belts would break and there'd be all kind of problems. Technic 1200s are direct drive; they have motors in 'em. They are very precise turntables.

Bringing Kurtis Blow out here, and him bringing out Davey DMX, changed the west coast forever. We were one of the first crews on the west coast to be officially able to scratch. I have to give Davey DMX from New York credit for taking the time out to teach DJ Yella how to scratch.

I decided at some point in time it might be good if I had a *house band* that would act like Run DMC. In fact, what we'd do was we would rap instead of playing instruments.

That was my first idea, to make a house band of rappers. I had a group of rappers in the club, and we made a record. It was called the EAD Rap. The EAD Rap was done to a song called "Rock, Skate, Roll, Bounce" by Vaughn Mason and Crew. We made the record, but I knew nothing about licensing, and the biggest fear I had in my life was a little line at the bottom of the record, right around the circle where it says, "This is a Federal property and protected by Federal copyrights."

The word "Federal" has always been intimidating to any Black man in the world. I just knew at some point in time the FBI was gonna come along, kick my door in and take me to jail for making this bootleg record! So the record never came out, but we made it and it made us popular. It moved us into what I call the "Bootleg Era."

The Bootleg Era

That gave me enough heart to start making underground records. They call them "mixtapes" today. They were not really mixed tape; they were actually mixed twelve-inches back then; now it's mixed CDs. Basically what it was—we would go in and mix a bunch of records together and we would sell them to record stores. This is where my record store connections came in and gave me the insight and the knowledge of how to go into the record store and sell the product.

Most of the record stores I would go to had never seen my face, but they knew my voice because we had a relationship over the phone. My voice and speech pattern are very distinctive. You wouldn't mistake my voice. If you talk to me, you know who I am. When I walked in, it was the first time most of them had ever laid eyes on me, but because they knew me by phone, they were very receptive to me selling them product. The records sounded good and they sold well.

My Bootleg Record Label

So that made for a great situation, and it made me a lot of money during the week. For the first time, I had a weekday income. Understand, Eve After Dark opened Friday and Saturday. So from Sunday to Thursday, I had nothing to do. I had money stashed. Everybody else I knew had a job, or went to school. My girlfriend went to work every day. I was just a young lonely baller. Nobody else I knew had my financial security, and I would try to find things to do. I decided to build a small studio in my house.

Part V

N.W.A.

"Music business makes strange bedfellows"
— Lonzo

32

Pre-N.W.A.: Jerry Heller and Our Major Record Deal

Before N.W.A., there was the World Class Wreckin' Cru. You gotta understand what led to the deconstruction of the Cru in order to really follow the creation of N.W.A.

We'll pick the story up with Jerry Heller. Jerry Heller was once one of the most influential managers in the music industry. He had represented Joan Armitrading, Elton John, and he was very well-respected in the music industry. I'm not sure what happened, but the time came when his career took a downfall and caused him a lot of personal problems.

In his book, he said he was semi-broke, living with his mom. He was on the comeback trail, and he and Maury Alexander would be in the hallway of Macola Records talking to various artists coming in, seeing the potential, follow their sales, whatever the case may be. They would talk to them about management and eventually signed quite a few artists out of there. Only a handful of artists became anybody of any notoriety. World Class Wreckin' Cru, Eazy E, L.A. Dream Team and Egyptian Lover were probably the primary acts that Jerry Heller or Maury Alexander signed that went on to do big things.

At one point while Wreckin' Cru was on tour, CBS called and offered us a record deal. I found out like this: One day while I was walking out of Macola, I met this cat named Petie. I only saw this guy twice in my life—before the CBS meeting and right after it...never again. I'm telling you, my life story is so crazy. I never saw this cat before anywhere.

"Hey man, you ever heard of Larkin Arnold?"

"Yeah! That's the guy that signed Frankie Beverly and Maze, Luther Vandross, Teena Marie and Michael Jackson—hell yeah, I know who he is!

"He wants to meet with you."

"Larkin wants to meet with me? Why?

"He thinks you guys got a good group, and he wants to meet with you."

The record business had like an unwritten rule that you couldn't go after somebody else's artist. There was no headhunting back then. At least, so we thought. Apparently, they sent Petie out to test it and see what would happen.

They knew we were independent. They had no idea we had our own labels, so when they found out we were independent, aw, they were happy. Not only did he ask for Wreckin' Cru, he called my boy Egyptian Lover, Arabian Prince, and Russ Parr.

I mentioned to Swamp Dog that CBS had called. We had just got off the road. We were gigging on a regular basis, getting our money from Macola, and we were doing pretty well. Swamp Dog was adamant…

"Man, don't sign with a major! You guys would do much bigger things independent…"

That made some sense to me. I got money, I got a house. I'd had money for a while, so it wasn't a big deal for me one way or the other. But I got three other guys who are still living with their moms. And because I considered the group somewhat of a limited partnership, they had some say. Swamp Dog had taught me a lot of things, but my guys weren't exposed to what I learned. All they knew was $100,000 was waiting for us and they got a chunk of that coming. So me being the group leader, they all had their arguments ready for me.

"Man, you already got money! Goddammit, I live at my momma's house! I wanna buy me a car…"

I tried not to go to CBS, but they wanted the money.

"Man, fuck that, we need to go, we need to do the deal, blah blah blah…"

"Man we need to do the deal! Do the deal! Do the deal!"

Swamp Dog did not like dealing with majors. He understood what I didn't understand. He understood that once you sign to a major, now you gotta stand in the assembly line. And you just don't have the freedom to do what I had been doing. Being independent, any time one of my records stopped selling, I just made another one. And the release date was when I got it finished! There was no schedule of releases at Kru-Cut Records. If the record finished on Tuesday, it came out on Wednesday—simple as that. Swamp Dog begged me not to sign.

"Man, please don't do it. *Please* don't do it. You'll have this $100,000 in six months anyway. Don't do it, don't do it..."

I did it anyway. Wreckin' Cru, Egyptian Lover, Arabian Prince, L.A. Dream Team, and Russ Parr all had meetings at CBS a half hour apart. Wreckin' Cru was the only one that got offered a deal that day. We were the first group on the west coast to sign to a major record deal. We are signed to CBS with Larkin Arnold as our executive producer. Now we are in the big time.

Before World Class Wreckin' Cru signed to CBS, Larkin asked me if I had any more groups. I told him yes. I remembered the group I had met at Dre's cousin Jinx's house called the Stereo Crew. Larkin gave them a single deal for a song Dre produced called "She's a Skag." I did that deal with just me and my lawyer, no manager—and saved us twenty percent.

I signed to Jerry Heller after I already had my CBS deals. Although I had met Jerry prior to the deal, I would not sign to him because it made no sense to me to give him twenty percent of $100,000 when basically negotiations were gonna be done between me and my lawyer anyway. He was gonna be the middleman between my lawyer and me to get me to approve the contract. So I figured without him in the middle, I'll save us $20,000, I'll deal with my lawyer direct—I bought a cell phone (back then it cost me $1,500 and it never left my car) so I was always available—and that's what I did.

I cut our CBS deal with my lawyer, who at that time was Ken Klavens, and it cost me about $7,500 bucks. So when we got through with our CBS deal, we had about $92,500 left over, as opposed to $72,000. *And* I have to point out for the math that although I was acting as the manager, I *didn't* take a management fee. I just took my regular cut from the group.

I saved us $20,000 (about five grand apiece, before expenses were taken out), but because my group members weren't as astute about business as I was, they never realized that. They never even appreciated the fact that I had enough sense to do that. They were so busy chasing girls, they left me with all the business, and every time something went wrong, they blamed *me*. Every time something went right, it was all about *we*. That's the basic philosophy of most artists.

Once the deal was signed, we received a partial advance of $10,000 with the balance due after the first of the year. Knowing we had $90,000 coming, the Cru immediately went into "lemme hold" mode. "I need $$ for this, lemme hold $$ for that..." Knowing how forgetful they were gonna be, I kept a record of every advance with a receipt book with their signatures on it, and I still have it to this day.

I don't think Jerry really liked that I had done the CBS deal before signing with him. He never seemed mad at me for doing it, but I kinda felt like although I was signed to him, Wreckin' Cru never got the same attention as other groups like LA. Dream Team. That was my personal feeling. Jerry told me that if he had negotiated the deal, it would have been different overall.

That CBS deal was probably the worst $100,000 I ever got in my life, because being signed to Epic, at this time we were behind Michael Jackson, Luther Vandross, Teena Marie—the best of the best. If an artist finished an album but a bigger artist finished their album at the same time, the bigger artist's album was released and the other artist got bumped. Our album was finished in February, but we got bumped back to July.

Hip hop was very spontaneous back then. Our stuff had always been trendy; we always tried to get ahead of the trend. Now, by the time we came out, the trend was over with! Our shit was stale.

Swamp Dog stepped away from us as management. He had taught me enough where I was able to use what he taught me to do the deal with just my lawyer, even though Jerry Heller was sitting there. Jerry knew I had enough sense, not saying he didn't have the connections, but I had enough sense to do some shit for myself. And because of this, I wasn't as amenable to some of the practices of the industry. Because of Swamp Dog's training, I had already been informed of what to look out for. So I didn't really need Jerry to do a lot of things that he did for everybody else. I wasn't a dumb artist anymore.

I don't think Swamp was mad; he was more disappointed more than anything, even though we were still cool. We still talked. I think I hurt him a little bit because he taught me so much. But I had been under so much pressure from the fellas to do the deal, so we did the deal.

As soon as the deal was done and it was no longer the dream we thought it was gonna be, their tune changed. The time came when the phone wasn't ringing. The Cru wasn't as popular as it was a year before when we signed to CBS. The Cru was complaining.

"How you gonna get us out of CBS?"

"Muthafucka, *say what*?"

"Man, we need to get out of this shit. We need to make some more records."

Now, the money's gone. They've bought cars; cars need gas. Beepers are turned off. Jheri Curls are dry. We're not gigging…shit's fucked up. I'm the only one that's got a couple dollars. Everybody's at my house every day, opening my refrigerator door looking for something.

Meantime, Dre's still getting tickets, still going to jail. He needed to get the fuck out of jail. I'm trying to finish the studio. I'm thinking we're gonna get a gig at any moment, but it ain't happening! We did a few small appearances, but it wasn't nothing like we were doing before the CBS deal.

When we were with Swamp Dog, we'd leave here Friday morning sometimes, broke, maybe a couple of dollars, and come back Monday morning with seven to ten grand to cut up! The rest of the week we'd mess around, rehearse, chase girls, whatever we gonna do, take care of business undercover… Next week, leave again! Come back with seven, eight, ten grand again.

It was a good time —we got spoiled. I didn't do as much stupid shit as they did, but I partied! And like most guys in the music game *and* the dope game, we didn't respect the money. We just acted a fool!

Nonetheless, our album was completed. As soon as we completed the album, Marketing asked us to duplicate one of the hottest songs of the time which was Free World by Jesse Johnson, a former member of the group "The Time." That's where The Fly stemmed from. We cut that track super-fast. Funny thing about The Fly is we kinda laughed at it. We just wanted to get a check and keep moving forward. That song over time became our most recognized song on the album!

We were put on hold for about four or five months. CBS gave us a small budget of about $10,000 to hire independent promoters to promote our album. I got the check I think on a Thursday. Friday, this big national story broke about how record companies are hiring independent promoters to deliver payola to radio stations!

Also during that time, the Senate Subcommittee had launched an investigation because of payola. That was a big thing, because they were saying that these guys were paying off these DJ's to play their records. So that was a two-pronged thing that we had to deal with. We couldn't get any promo for our album and then these DJ's were afraid of what was going on with this subcommittee investigation, so it was just a bad time.

Record Promotion

Payola has always been a necessary no-no. It's always been a part of the game, but it's always been quiet and under the table, and everybody can't deliver it. It's like, you got to know who to know to get what you want done.

All program directors like different things—some want cash, some want coke, some want girls, some want you to do a free gig. And based on your relationship with the program directors at the various radio stations, you had to come up with these different things to get your record played.

One of the best guys in the country was gonna promote our single. He was actually interested in doing the whole album. Next thing I know, he's on the goddamn news accused of being the head of a national payola ring, with alleged connections to the Mafia! Oh my God! People talk that shit about the record industry and the Mafia—I *know* what's happening! This news only meant one thing—the meeting I had just had with him was a wrap, the deal was not happening.

So we got the ten grand and we can't use it for independent promotion. I asked Jerry, "What do we do with the ten grand?" He said spend it, so I cut it up with the fellas.

Now we didn't have any promotion on our products because of the crackdown on independent record promoters. And of course nobody knows anything, hands are in pockets and faces are up to the sky, saying *I don't have a clue about any of this.* So we had an album with no promotions. We were sitting on our hands pretty much not doing anything.

My House

By now, thanks to a lead from Etta James, I had a new house with a better studio in it. Etta James was one of the people whose lawns dad cut on weekends. She was a good friend of the family.

My brother kept Etta abreast of what I was doing, and Etta would give me advice through my brother. A house became available in Etta's neighborhood; it was owned by Johnny Otis. Etta knew I was getting a record deal, knew I had the money.

> "Tell your brother, Lonzo, he needs to come buy Johnny Otis' house."

Johnny Otis was a big-time blues singer. Johnny had done what I hope to have happen to me one day. He owned his catalog of music —I don't think he knew that those records would change his life the way they did.

A movie studio contacted him about licensing his music catalog for the movie they were producing at the time, which was "Back to The Future", and the rest is history. Before he sold me the house, he had just added a full-fledged studio to it. All that was left for me to do was to upgrade it with up-to-date equipment. I remember what Etta told me...

"Boy, this is a nice, big-ass house with a studio in it, don't be no fool and miss out..."

If you knew Etta, she had a way of making you feel stupid if you didn't do the obvious, and I never liked feeling stupid. The house was in a neighborhood I was very familiar with because as a kid, I had cut lawns with my dad in that neighborhood for years on both sides of that house, and sometimes Johnny's house as well.

I remember as a kid, cutting my now neighbor's yard, pulling up in the yard and hearing the band playing next door through the wall. I never knew that one day I would own that house.

Etta always had her way of giving advice. She'd say things like,

"Hey, watch yourself with your new management. I don't know Jerry, but I do know Maury. Don't be surprised if you play with a snake and he bites your ass!"

Non-stop House Party

It's 1986 and I'm in my new house; the World Class Wreckin' Cru is the shit. New studio, new equipment. We're doing parties at Skateland when we're not gigging. And everybody's at Lonzo's house—I'm talking *everybody*—the who's who of the future of West Coast hip hop. I'm talking about DJ Pooh, Coolio, Easy E, an eleven-year-old Warren G, Body and Soul—a girl group that consisted of Rose, one of Dre's friends, and Dee Barnes—just to name a few. Everyone would chill, write lyrics, and play songs they had recorded here or elsewhere.

I'd have record store owners stopping by to hear what we were doing in the studio and sometimes they would just hang out. Not to mention I had a Jacuzzi that always had someone in it. It was like a non-stop music video.

When we weren't recording, rehearsing, or hanging out, we had girls everywhere. Without going into details, let's just say we had special girls. As Yella would say, *"Cathy's back in town."*

33

Reckless to Ruthless

It can be reckless to be too giving.

Eric came to me for consultation about starting Ruthless Records. He was seeking advice on how to get the company off the ground, how to get the records played, and how to manufacture them. I taught him how to do everything necessary to make a record; I also introduced him to my lawyer, Kent Klavens who did his contracts, my graphic designer Darryl, and Donavan who owned the recording studio Audio Achievements in Torrance. Then he started bugging me to meet Greg Mack from KDAY, and later Jerry Heller.

While Easy was putting together Ruthless Records, the world Class Wreckin' Cru and Stereo Crew were still signed to CBS. When Eric asked me about taking a tape to Larkin Arnold, our executive producer, I was like, *"Man, they'll toss me out the fifth story window for trying to sell an NAACP member a group named Niggaz With Attitude!"*

When the concept of N.W.A. was being developed, I couldn't feel the name. World Class Wreckin' Cru had just gone through a bunch of shit about saying "ass" on the end of our record "House Calls." We had to edit it down to "a" and still got sweated.

Shakespeare...

"When N.W.A. first started out, it wasn't no gangsta rap—it was Arabian Prince who was another local guy, and they did the song called Panic Zone, and it was like that wasn't nothin' but Wreckin' Cru right there.

I think these guys who came from New York were the ones who kinda steered 'em in the gangsta direction, because they wanted something edgier, and then that's when Ice Cube came up with "Boyz in the Hood."

Back in the day Dre's number one line was *"I gotta get paid."* We all would sit around talking about how we could make money. Luther "Uncle Luke" Campbell, known back then as "Luke Skywalker," had just been sued and it was all over the news. He had released a song on Macola call M.F.S.B. and the lawsuit made that song fly off the shelves.

It became obvious that controversy sold records. We thought that the biggest controversy was sex, and Luke and the 2 Live Crew had that covered. What could be done to spark that kinda of controversy? What was gonna be the next big thing?

Boyz in the Hood

Eazy was not the original artist for the Boyz in the Hood project. He had been hanging out with Dre and saw how we were making money selling records to the various swap meets and stores, and he wanted to get into the record business. He had a pretty good rap artist named Rendezvous that he was gonna put on his record label. Rendezvous read the contract, didn't understand it, and decided that he wanted to do something else.

HBO was a group out of New York. They looked like Run DMC. HBO stood for Home Boys Only. They were also supposed to do tracks for Eazy, but it didn't work out. The track they were supposed to do was Boyz in the Hood. They didn't feel Dre's beats and they couldn't relate to the lyrics, so they didn't wanna do it.

There we were…Eazy had these tracks he paid for, with nobody to rap on.

"Hey man, go on and cut your track," Dre told Eazy. "Do it yourself!"

Reluctantly, Eazy did the track. *Reluctantly.* We're sitting in my house—again, my house was the Mecca of west coast hip hop—and Dre comes in the house after few hours giggling and laughing.

"Check this out! Check out Eric!"

We put the track in the stereo—it's Boyz in the Hood!

> "Boyz in the Hood, it's always hard
> You come talkin' that crap and we'll pull your card…"

Everybody fell out laughing! The verse was like, *no way!*

> "Nah dude," I told 'em, "y'all not understanding! Don't laugh! Stranger things have happened! Guys with less talent have become big artists!"

One of the major stars in hip hop was Biz Markie. He wasn't the greatest rapper in the world, and then Eric comes along with his squeaky voice. Contrary to the movie I was the only one that didn't diss the song. And of course, Eazy ultimately did blow up.

Eazy wants to get the record to KDAY, to Greg Mack. Everybody knows me and Greg have a relationship. He wants to get this record to Greg, but Greg can't play it 'cause of the cussing. Eazy finally takes the cussing out and gets it to Greg; in the meantime, Eazy's bugging me to get to Jerry Heller.

Dre has hyped up Jerry Heller to Eazy like he is the godfather of music simply because Jerry helped us get some money that was missing from a payment. When we had our CBS deal, although they owed us $92,000, they only paid us about $86,000. We couldn't figure out where the rest of the money went, so I told Jerry Heller what happened. We told Jerry we were missing about six grand. He was like, "Let me look into it."

Jerry looked into it and he found out that AFTRA had withheld the money for union dues. Although we weren't in the AFTRA union, they still withheld it 'cause CBS is a union house. Jerry told us what to do and we went in and got the money. He sent us down to AFTRA, we had to sign off and go Taft-Hartley, and we were able to get our money. With that move, Jerry officially became our manager. He and his partner Maury already managed The L.A. Team and The Egyptian Lover; with World Class Wreckin' Cru, he had most of the heavy hitters in L.A.

34

"Fuck the Police," Again
What I Remember

When the Cru was together, we all used to be into paint ball. I thought paint ball was gonna be the answer to gang banging, because here you had a chance to shoot at another sonofabitch, hit him, and it wouldn't kill him. I thought it might be a way to get out some frustration and have a good time.

Little did I know Dre and Eazy would take this sport and get crazy with it on the freeway and end up in one of the situations that contributed to their decision to produce their anthem, "Fuck the Police."

Dre, Yella, Rudy, Russ Parr, and I all got into paint ball. We had paint ball guns, camouflage gear, masks, the whole nine

206

yards. And almost every Saturday, we'd travel to Malibu and shoot at white boys with paint balls! We were the only Blacks out there. In fact, we called our crew "Just Us."

We were notorious because we were so damn fast, they couldn't shoot us! They played like it was football—you had to get the flag and get back to your ground with their flag in order for you to win the game. We set up a perimeter around a guy, get the flags by running and shooting, and usually we'd win! It got to the point that we got so bad, when we showed up, the white boys didn't want us all on the same team. They made us break our team up because we were kicking so much ass playing paintball.

Eazy wanted to play with us also. He had a few dollars, so he went and bought himself a paintball shotgun. I can never recall him going with us to Malibu, but Eazy always had this paintball shotgun when he'd come to my house!

One day Eazy and Dre, and I don't remember who else, decided they were gonna ride down the Harbor Freeway, stick this paintball shotgun out the window and shoot at people's cars. Between my house and the 405, there's a Highway Patrol station right off the goddamn freeway! These young crazy fools were riding down the Harbor Freeway sticking the shotgun out the goddamn car and "POW"—shoot a big-ass red splot—you don't know if you've been shot or not! You're not sure!

People are pulling off the road, driving erratically, cops don't know what's happening. They see these fools, they pull them over, they put guns to their heads, they almost *kill* 'em...today, they would'a been DEAD. They would have been shot and killed.

They come back to my house shaking like leaves on a tree on a windy day, damn near crying.

"Man, fuck the police! Them muthafuckas ..."

I said, "Are you serious?"

"They didn't have to do us like that!"

"Are you **SERIOUS?** A paintball shotgun ***looks like a shotgun***! You stuck a paintball shotgun out the car, shootin' at cars, and you wonder why the cops treated y'all like that?"

They kicked them around, handcuffed them, roughed them up pretty tough, and they came back to the house pissed off, scared, and lucky to be alive. I'm sitting and listening to them tell the story.

"And the cops were wrong, right?"

"Yeah, fuck them muthafuckas! Fuck the police! Them muthafuckas ain't shit!"

So when I first heard the record "Fuck the Police," that's the first incident that came to my mind. After the beating and verdict in the Rodney King case, that song was the national anthem of street soldiers. N.W.A. was pissed off, and now they had the ear of the public. They could say *"fuck the police,"* and people who had been fucked with by the police—like myself—felt their sentiment.

35

Eric "Eazy E" Wright

I briefly met Eric at the Eve After Dark. The first night he came with Dre and I refused them entry because of the way they were dressed. The next time he showed up, I refused him entry for the same reason. He eventually got into the club and hung out from time to time. He was about 5'5" and talked the most shit. Eric made his height, voice, and mannerisms work for him—he was a funny dude. When he came to my house he was driving a Suzuki Samurai. When he got out of the car, the first thing I noticed was his eye was black as hell. He kept holding it.

"What happened to you?"

Dre said his girl had hit him with a GI Joe lunch pail— *fucked* him up!

Eric was a nice guy, but his girl at the time had him on a short leash! He had to report to her on every move he made. This dude had to use my phone and report in every time he got to my house!

"Yeah, I'm over Lonzo's house. Dre, Yella…Lonzo, he's in the kitchen…"

Then he'd hang up. When we left the house…

"We fittin' to leave. Uh, we going to Macola. I'm driving my car. Lonzo's gonna drive his BMW. Nah, it ain't no girls, it's just the fellas."

And later…

"Oh, we going to Pink's Hotdogs. I'ma get a hotdog with chili. I'ma get me a Coke. I might get some…"

Used to drive us fucking nuts! Everywhere the fuck we'd go, he had to stop and check in!

"Man, *what are you doin'?*"

"Aw, man, I don't wanna hear her mouth. She be trippin' sometime."

Back then we only had cordless phones in the house and it had gotten so bad that every time I wanted to use my phone

I had to find Eric because he'd have it in his pocket. That shit drove me nuts. I'm like, God*damn!*

Looking back at the ultra-gangsta N.W.A. days, it's amazing how the world was affected and a generation was changed by such nice guys just playing a part. I know what I just said may seem like telling people there ain't no Santa Claus. When you tell a kid there's no Santa Claus, the kid won't get mad at the person who told them the lie that there *was* a Santa Claus. He's gonna get mad at the one who told him there's really *no* Santa Claus.

Unlike most people, I knew the members of N.W.A. except Ren before they turned into their characters and put on a Raiders hats. Some people will mistake this as me coming off as a hater—not the case at all, but anybody that knows me knows I'm a straight shooter and I keep it at 100 all the time. So when I say certain things, it's not to hurt anybody's image; it's just to help somebody not to be influenced by lyrics and a stage persona. Hopefully a young person will understand that the imagery that was created was more of an act than the true person. Like an alter ego.

If you've ever been backstage at a play, you see the actors before they put on their makeup, you see them before they hit the stage, so when you're backstage of a production, your perception is totally different from anybody else's. When you're in the audience, you see the finished product.

All you know is the finished product. All you care to see is the finished product. But there are various sides to every production—preproduction, production and postproduction. I know the preproduction. I lived backstage.

Eazy and Jerry Heller

When Jerry assisted us in getting our $1,500 each from AFTRA, as far as Dre and Yella were concerned, Jerry Heller was a god. So the next thing you know, Dre's hyped Jerry up to Eric and Eric wants to meet him.

The way Jerry tells the story in his book, he met Eric through me, which is true. Where our two stories differ is that Jerry claims he was so impressed with Eric and his music that he felt like my crew and I, who were established artists, should be a part of Eric's new unproven crew. If we decided not to, he wasn't going to deal with us anymore. And Jerry said Eazy paid me $750.00 dollars to meet him.

Here's what really happened. Dre was doing beats for Eazy in exchange for Eazy bailing him out of jail that time I was gonna let him stay in for a while and think about not getting speeding tickets left and right. Dre used my studio to do Eric's beats. I explained to Dre and Eazy both that *Dre* went to jail, Lonzo didn't, so using the studio came with a cost. Dre programming Eazy's beats, that was on Dre.

"I'll let him use my drum machine, but when he pushes 'Record,' I need to get paid."

Eazy racked up about $500 in studio time doing his demos. When Eazy told me he wanted to meet Jerry Heller, he owed me for all that studio time, and I told him I wasn't introducing him to *no*body 'til I got my money.

Eric was notorious for wanting to give you crumbs, $15 or $20 at time on a debt, like you'd do a crackhead. He'd be walking around looking like he was wearing an ankle monitor because he'd have all this money in his sock. He would cry broke all the time because he never had money in his pockets. He always kept it in his sock, and if he wanted something, he'd go to the sock and pull it out; but if you ask him for *your* money, he'd pat his pockets and cry broke.

"No, go to your sock and give me my goddamn money!"

"Look," he said, "I'ma give you your money, but if you hook me up with Jerry Heller, I'll kick in an extra $250 if you can do it by Wednesday.

"Okay, cool." That worked for me.

Eazy paid his studio bill, which was $500, and he gave me an extra $250 to get me to expedite the meeting. So I called

214

Jerry and told him that I had this guy that wanted to meet him. It took me a couple of tries to get Jerry to meet with Eazy.

"Look man, this guy owes me some money and he wants to meet you. Take the meeting with him. I'd appreciate it…"

Jerry said, "For you, I'll meet him."

And that's what happened. I gotta be honest, I didn't think that Eazy and Jerry would pan out. I mean, they were from two different worlds. When Jerry did meet Eazy, he didn't think much of him. He came to me.

"Hey man, what you think about this thing?"

"I don't know, dude, it's a'ight. But it's going to be controversial because of the amount of times he uses the words bitch and hoe."

Besides that, the name was just crazy and it had cussing and the whole nine yards. Jerry was very concerned about the whole cussing aspect of it. He tells the story like he thought Eazy was a goddamn genius. That's not quite true! He was so used to dealing with cats like me, Rudy, Egypt—we were all from the 80's but we were businessmen.

We wore business casual clothes and dress shoes every day; we wore slacks. You might catch me in a sport coat.

Egypt wore suits all the damn time. We had brief cases and knew how to conduct basic business. Eric walked around in Levis and tennis shoes and a white tee-shirt, you know. That was his thing. So it was a whole different mannerism. We were both from Compton, but we were from two different eras.

Jerry seemed reluctant to deal with Eric at first. He damn sure wasn't sure about the music, and he **damn** sure was really confused about the name Niggaz With Attitude. He expressed his concern.

> "You know I'm a Jewish guy, and you guys calling it Niggaz With Attitude—what do I do, how do I do this?

> I said to him, "Very carefully."

That's why *I* didn't mess with it. I'm dealing with heavy hitters in the music industry—Larkin Arnold, Jheryl Busby—I mean, these are my mentors. I can't tell Larkin Arnold, an NAACP member, "Hey man, I got a group called Niggaz With Attitude; we have to sign 'em." And Jheryl Busby, one of the most respected black men in the music industry! I can't take him no group named Niggaz With Attitude! They'd throw me out the goddamn building!

Truthfully speaking, Jerry had no idea what he had; neither did the owner of Priority Records, Brian. But on the same token, Jerry was the best person for Eric to work with. I know for a fact that if *I* had tried to sell them to Larkin Arnold or any other Black executives that I knew in the industry, they would have had my ass on a skewer barbequing at the next NAACP meeting.

But because it was a non-Black power machine that put it out there with Eric and N.W.A. out front being the focal point, if it blew up in a negative way, they could deflect and absorb any negative blowback. And if it blew up in a positive way, everybody could reap the benefits. It all depended on the public reaction. As we all know, it started off rough.

Eric had the ability to adapt to his character Easy E. He was great at playing his role—a young, crazy, ex-dope-dealer-made-good. Again his size and natural ability to talk big shit made it interesting. He was like a modern-day James Dean. If you knew Eric like I did, you knew that wasn't him. He was actually kinda of a quiet, laid back guy.

36

O'Shea "Ice Cube" Jackson

While recording demos for World Class Wreckin' Cru, I came across Stereo Cru, which consisted of O'Shea "Ice Cube" Jackson, Tony "Sir Jinx" Wheatob & Darryl "KD" Johnson. When I met them, they were all youngsters around fifteen years old. O'Shea and Stereo Crew would be around my house. O'Shea was always writing, always coming up with new ways to deliver his lyrics. Sometimes he would run them past me.

Unfortunately, my mind most of the time was on running Kru-Cut records. Looking back, I realize I never gave him the attention he deserved at that time. Although we never had any problems, we were on different planes because I was so much older. O'Shea never swole up, never stepped out of line, was always respectful—always was a cool kid. Unlike Jinx who used to work my nerves to no end because he played so much;

he was always dancing and had a quick wit. KD was the coolest. He never said much, but he was always clean. Oddly enough, all three guys in Stereo Crew were Geminis like myself. That's probably why I liked them so much.

Stereo Crew was the first group I signed to CBS as part of our deal with Larkin Arnold. It was a single deal for a song called "She's a Skag," a Beastie Boy-ish imitation at that time. In fact, most of the songs that Stereo Crew aka CIA recorded for Kru-Cut were imitations of the Beastie Boys' flow. While on Kru-Cut, Stereo Crew and CIA made very little noise in the industry, if any at all. After their record didn't sell, they were dropped from CBS and later from Kru-Cut.

After his time with Kru-Cut Records, O'Shea left to go to college. When he came home for summer vacation, that's when he hooked up with Dre and them and joined N.W.A. Shortly after that, I heard he had left the group. I was surprised when O'Shea left N.W.A., but he wasn't the first member to leave N.W.A.—Arabian Prince was, but he left without any ill feelings. In fact, he turned around and brought J.J. F.A.D. and their hit "Supersonic" to Ruthless records.

When O'Shea left, though, there *were* ill feelings. When a Benedict Arnold (traitor) reference was made in a song toward him, it was *on* and he came back with "No Vaseline"—he told the whole story and ripped their *asses* out one by one. He retaliated in such a prolific way, they had to end that beef real quick.

In the movie "Straight Outta Compton," for the first time in decades I heard the word "Jew" in No Vaseline in its correct context. That scene went over big in the theatre— most people never heard it on the record; it was always reversed or beeped out. I was *totally* surprised by this! I'm glad they kept it real.

Also, that night at the after-party, for the first time since he left to go to college, I was able to lay eyes on O'Shea face to face. We hadn't talked in over twenty-five years. When he saw me, his face lit up in surprise and he gave me a hug and a look of sincerity.

"Lonzo, I wanna thank you for allowing us to be at your house, man, and lettin' us hang around you. You inspired us in ways you don't even know. We were just knucklehead kids hanging around your house trying to make music, and this is what it turned out to be. I just wanna thank you, man to man."

And he gave me another hug. We took a picture together for the first time. I was touched by that brief meeting. I felt what he was saying; I felt his sincerity. Just like when I saw Dre for the first time in twenty years while the movie was shooting...I felt a sense of pride to have had such a powerful influence. I'm proud of all of them.

One thing I can say is when O'Shea left Kru-Cut, he and Brian took care of business in a professional way. I received a call at home from Brian. He explained to me that O'Shea had left N.W.A. and was recording a solo project and was taking his career in different direction from what he had done on Kru-Cut and that he wanted to buy the CIA masters. Without much more conversation, he made a nice offer and I accepted it. The next day I delivered the masters, got paid, and we both moved on.

37

Kim "Arabian Prince" Nazel

Prior to becoming a member of NWA, Arabian Prince was a local independent artist with a solo career, and performing with groups like Bobby Jimmy and the Critters. He also produced JJ Fad's super hit "Supersonic." He was already a legendary staple in the west coast hip hop community.

The name Niggaz With Attitude (N.W.A.) was conceived in Arabian Prince's living room. He became part of N.W.A. in the very early stages. He was a producer of some of their popular dance songs, Panic Zone and Something to Dance To.

Arabian was an electrofunk music producer like Egyptian Lover and World Class Wreckin' Cru. He gave N.W.A. the dance tracks that were very popular at that time. He was featured on their first album and you'll see him in most of the early photoshoots. Knowing Arabian like I do, I know he was never really into the gangsta rap per se; that's never been his forté.

Arabian was the first member of the group to leave, before Ice Cube, for contractual and money issues. JJ Fad was originally on Dream Team Records, and was the first group to be picked up by Ruthless for their Atlantic distribution deal.

Although Arabian left Ruthless and sued, they still maintained a cool relationship. Unfortunately, he wasn't mentioned in the movie "Straight Outta Compton." I'm sure his upcoming media projects will explain why.

38

Lorenzo "MC Ren" Patterson

MC Ren was probably the only member of N.W.A. that I have no recollection of having any interaction with. He became a part of N.W.A. after they were no longer hanging out at my house. If he spent any time at my house, he was so quiet I didn't know who he was.

39

Ultimatum

Shortly after I introduced Eric and Jerry, and Jerry began working with Eric, and the west coast heavy hitters (myself, Egypt, Rudy, and Unknown) had some concerns we felt we needed to express to Jerry regarding the images of his new client. Jerry needed to make a decision—either us or Eric.

The day came when we had to have this big meeting. There was a restaurant on Cahuenga called Martoni's. Martoni's was a Mafia-style restaurant. It was an Italian restaurant, and it looked like a scene out of The Godfather. We had reserved this little room in the back of the restaurant that was reserved for private meetings. I understood that some of the biggest deals in Hollywood had been cut in this room. The room was small. The table was huge—might have held about 15 people back there. It was separate from the regular restaurant. If you knew somebody, you could get in the back room at Martoni's. I liked it because it reminded me of some old Mafia shit.

So we're at Martoni's. It's myself, Unknown DJ, Rudy from the Dream Team, Egyptian Lover, Atron Gregory, Lisa of Egyptian Empire, and Jerry Heller. Lisa and Unknown DJ are pretty much the spokespersons for the conversation, although Unknown was the only one at the table not managed by Jerry. This meeting led to our collectively giving Jerry the ultimatum. We were calling Jerry on the carpet for representing Eazy E and N.W.A. We don't like it! We don't like what they represent! We let him know from the very beginning that we weren't feeling it.

I wasn't as vocal as everybody else was since these guys came out of my camp. I couldn't really be like, *"Fuck Eazy, forget the whole situation..."* I couldn't do that because I would be a double-hypocrite. They did the shit in my studio. I had hooked Jerry up with Eric. I'm also the man behind West Coast record distributors. I'm stuck in the middle of all this shit. I considered myself a facilitator. I facilitated various situations.

So I'm sitting here feeling like I'm stuck in the middle, mainly because I know all the players and Jerry is still my manager. Unknown, Rudy, and Lisa really led the meeting and put Jerry on notice. They were very direct and up-front about what they needed to say. Basically, they gave him an ultimatum, *"It's either us or Eazy E."* I didn't totally agree with them on this. For the most part, I dealt more with Atron Gregory, who was also Tupac's and Digital Underground's manager. By this time, Atron and I had become buddies. Jerry kinda had everybody on hold while he worked closely with N.W.A., but Jerry was trying to show us the benefits of him representing all of us on the West Coast. He felt it would have given him more power and that would be to all our benefits. Rudy, Egypt and Lisa expressed our concerns to Jerry.

"That's not what we're about! We don't need that type of situation attached to us. The whole bitches and hoe's thing, we ain't with that. We live in the community where this stuff affects you. We see the effects of this kind of stuff. You don't! So we can't have you perpetuating this in our community."

That's how we felt about it. That was the sentiment. That day, Jerry had to make a decision whether he was gonna stick with us or go with Eric. In his book, he made it seem like he met Eric on Tuesday and cut ties with us on Wednesday. *Not the case!* Not the case at all. He wanted to be the king of the entire west coast; manage the whole west coast. That would make him a super-player, because if anybody had a hit record, he could always put us on tours together. We didn't go for it.

I had to clarify that because it's really amazing how different people see the same situation. And whoever speaks out on it first, usually that's who people believe.

So yes, we called the meeting with Jerry Heller at Martoni's, gave him the ultimatum—*you're either working with them, or you're working with us*—and he chose them. Nobody was mad, nobody had any regrets. We all went on to do our own thing.

Part VI

Team Wreckin' Cru

In early years of the Wreckin' Cru, I had no idea what I was doing so I was always looking for guidance. Like most young men, I couldn't let it be known that I was ignorant to the game, but unlike most youngsters today, I wasn't too proud to listen when someone dropped some knowledge on me. The only problem was that like most rookies to any game, I didn't know knowledge from bullshit. The next few chapters discuss a few of the people that had an impact on my life and the careers of the World Class Wreckin' Cru with both knowledge and bullshit.

40

Shirley

I forgot where I met Shirley. Somebody turned me on to her. Her dad was a big time blues singer. If you ever see the movie *Cadillac Records*, there's a character portraying him in that movie. Shirley's dad had a lot of money. He had publishing money coming and his daughter, Shirley, allegedly helped him recover his publishing money.

Shirley saw us at a show someplace and approached me and the fellas about being somebody who might wanna relieve me of the management responsibilities. I was doing it all—I was trying to rehearse, trying to chase Macola down, I had a social life, I had a daughter…I had things going on. I was doing too much. If I could find somebody to take the helm of management, it would take a little stress off me.

So Shirley comes into the picture. She talked a great game. She was from Chicago, and she sounded like she knew more than I did. She knew more terminology and she dropped names that were familiar. She had us convinced that she could help us take our career to the next level, because she supposedly had been very instrumental as a manager for her father. At some point Shirley developed a crush on me.

Shirley was not my type. I had a girl at the time. My girl saw her coming. She was like, *"Nah, that bitch ain't right."* Shirley had a couple of younger sisters that came to my shows; they had their eyes on Dre and Yella. I think they all had plans for somebody in the group.

Photo Shoot for First Album

It was about 1984 when we shot our first record cover. Prince was the man that was hot on the scene. That's when eyeliner, lace and Jheri curls were the idea. Shirley thought that we should embrace it; basically, she wanted to pretty us up just a little bit. She gave me and Cli-N-Tel a little eyeliner and we were cool, but Dre went with the lip gloss and the blush and the eyeliner. Yella did too, including his lace glove—he really thought he was little Prince, but that's another subject. Shirley's plan was to make us compatible with groups like Ready for the World and acts in the same genre. But Shirley was tricking us already.

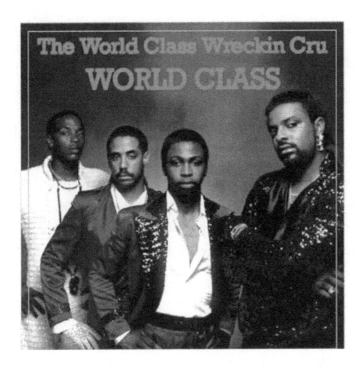

"We got $25,000 from Macola," Shirley tells us. "I just cashed the check. Look, give me $4,000. I'm going to get you guys an ad in Ebony and Jet."

As you very well know, up to that time Ebony and Jet had been two prestigious magazines that had been around forever. I would *love* to be in Ebony *or* Jet. This was prior to the shit going down about the $300,000 lie. So, I took a little vote.

"Hey, what y'all wanna do? We got an album coming out. Give her the money?"

"Yeah, give her the money! Give her the money!"

Gave her the $4,000. Never heard from her about that again.

> "Oh, we're gonna do that…it'll take about 90 days,
> I'll be in touch…"

We don't know. We're dumb—stupid.

After the photo shoot, she left and went back to Chicago. She was supposed to place these ads that we never saw, and now everybody's wondering what happened to Shirley and the four grand that we gave her. We tried contacting her. There was no answer.

These guys had already started grumbling among themselves toward me; now they're grumbling to me about her. What do I do? We *all* voted for her to be our manager. We *all* voted to give her the $4,000, but now that something was going wrong, all the fingers are pointing at *me*, and I'm like, *I didn't do this shit by myself!*

Shirley got us one gig as World Class Wreckin' Cru in Pittsburgh, California. I didn't know there was a Pittsburgh, California! So we pull up to the gig, and we see our name on the marquee:

> **"Welcome Dr. Dre and the
> World Class Wreckin' Cru"**

That was the biggest shock we'd ever had! That was the first time we'd ever seen our name in lights. And that was the first and only time we were ever "**Dr. Dre and** the World Class Wreckin' Cru!" How in the hell did we become that?

Shirley and her sisters traveled with us. What I didn't know—because most of the time on the bus, I was asleep— was that in the back of the bus, a little orgy was allegedly going down, including Shirley, her sisters, Dre, Yella, and Cli-N-Tel. When we got back to L.A., I was trying to find a way to keep Shirley in the mix without firing her, but she was causing so much havoc between me and the Cru, she was making it real difficult to keep working with her.

We were playing a big show one night in the Long Beach Arena, and I met a girl backstage that caught my eye. Her name was Michelle. She was friends with one of the Force MD's. We talked and we hung out.

Our elusive manager shows up to the show, sees me with this new young lady and gets an attitude. My first thought was where are our ads or our money, but I didn't trip because we had just had a good show and we were in Long Beach at home. I got my new BMW. I'm having a good time. I'm making money. I'm a star in my own mind. And I just made a new friend, so what the hell.

Anyway, since I was in Long Beach, I took Michelle home with me that night and we hung out. No big deal, right away.

Well, shortly thereafter, my guys and I start having problems. I hadn't done anything to them, but they started to trip a little bit, saying little shit and making comments, being funny…but they always were kinda weird, so I didn't really pay it much attention.

That was a mistake.

At some point, I get a letter from Dance Fever, a television show taped in Hollywood. A dance group wants to perform to one of our records in a championship dance-off. The song was called "Juice" off our album. It was an up-tempo dance cut, and it was a good song. Dance Fever offered me $300 to let them use "Juice" on this particular show, with residuals, of course.

When they made me that offer, I took it to my manager Shirley's attention. I had no idea what publishing was. I had heard of copyrights—I didn't really know what they did for you, but because my lawyer at the time had made sure I had the copyrights, I owned the publishing, and because I was the financier of the group, everything was pretty much in my name.

I had no idea this was going to turn out to be one of the biggest nightmares of my career. As Michelle and I got closer, Shirley and I were getting farther apart—but I also noticed that my group members were getting closer to her.

I did the deal for $300 with Dance Fever right before we got ready to go on tour. Mona Lisa, her daughter Charity, and Boss Hog had shown up and we were waiting for Dre, Yella and Cli-N-Tel to arrive so we could hit the road to Mississippi. We had packed up all the equipment the night before. The Cru never showed up.

I got a tour bus waiting. Everybody's on standby. All the beepers I had bought and paid for to keep in touch with everybody—nobody was responding to my phone calls. A day of travel time had passed by and not a word. Later that evening, I heard from Greg Mack. He had talked to the fellas and he told me about some issues they had with me that I was not aware of. They were upset with me because they felt I had pulled some fucked up shit.

Seems Shirley went from having a crush on Lonzo to her lying ass telling Dre, Yella and Cli-N-Tel that Dance Fever gave me **$300-*thousand***, and that I had bought an apartment building in Compton, bought all kinda stuff, and they didn't get any money. In fact, she was so pissed off at me, she told them that she was going back to Chicago to hire a lawyer to sue me on their behalf. She instructed them not to talk to me in the meantime, and then she did not talk to me at all when she got back in town.

I laughed at first, it was so ridiculous. Nonetheless, it was told to them by Shirley, who had gained their trust despite having lied to them several times in the past. So now I have people waiting, the bus is burning fuel, and time is passing. I decided to grab some stand-in dudes for the gig and we headed for Mississippi. I was hoping to teach them the songs and rehearse them enough on the bus so they'd be ready in time to do the show.

Well, old Murphy's Law stepped in and everything that could go wrong did go wrong. It was miserable—we were stuck in a bus with no air conditioning. I'm working with two look-alikes. We tried. The bus broke down. They couldn't get us another bus out there; couldn't get us to the arena. It was hot as hell. This was one of those situations when I was glad we didn't make it. I tried to rehearse these guys on the bus. Couldn't do it; it was just too hot. The air conditioning went out in Arizona and we could hardly function. It was 110 degrees outside and we were on a bus! It was horrible. Then the brakes went out in Texas.

We didn't get to Mississippi 'til the day after the show. By the time we get to Mississippi our names are Mud. We missed the show entirely. We were the headliners of the show; Ready for the World was our opening act. We never showed up. We looked like clowns, assholes, the whole nine yards.

When we got there, we had to go on the radio and apologize. The radio station was dissing us on the air. It was a radio station promotion, and the guy at the radio station who had actually promoted the show, the jock, was pissed at us to no end. I mean he was PISSED. He didn't wanna say shit to me. He didn't want to look at me.

This was not working. The only thing that saved us was my secret weapon—my singer, Mona Lisa. You have to see Mona Lisa to appreciate her assets. The key word here is *ass*-ets. Mona Lisa has an ass that will not quit.

> "Mona, I need you to make this guy smile. He ain't feeling us worth a damn. He's gonna pull our record off the radio and everything else."

When I sent her into the radio station wearing some of the tightest pants that she could possibly slide onto this enormous monument of womanhood, it was all over. Everything changed. Everything. I didn't say shit else. She talked to him. She apologized for us, blah blah blah. He's all grins, all teeth, all happy. They forgot about the concert. They forgot about me. They forgot about us not showing up. All eyes on the ass. We do the interview. We apologize to Mississippi, tell them we're coming back, and everything was cool. It was just amazing.

Now I got a bigger problem. I gotta get back to L.A. and get my original crew back. I told my road manager, Boss Hog Randy Ran, I was going back to get my fellas. We went back to get Dre and them. I caught a plane back to L.A.; everybody else rode back on the bus. When I got back to L.A., I tracked Dre down at a party.

"Man, what the hell's going on?" I ask Dre.

"Aw man, I heard…

"Dude, I didn't do that …"

I told him what happened.

"Look, man, Shirley done ripped us all off. I got a new manager. He's much better. He's booking gigs for us left and right. We got money we could be making out here. Let's go get our money."

"Yeah."

I tell Dre, fuck Yella 'cause he should know better, but Dre tells me he ain't going unless Yella goes. What could I do?

"Go get Yella. Let's go."

Well, now I got my two boys, Yella and Dre, my main characters, but Cli-N-Tel is holding out. He doesn't want to come back. He's still under Shirley's influence. She had told them not to talk to me for any reason whatsoever, and that she would be back to town to handle the business of getting their fair share of World Class Wreckin' Cru. Well, that was back in 1985. I've never seen or heard from this woman again in life.

So Cli-N-Tel stayed with Shirley. He left after World Class Wreckin' Cru's debut album, "World Class." When we signed with Epic Records (CBS), Shakespeare was now the MC. Epic had also signed Stereo Cru (aka CIA). We proceeded to release more singles and our second album, "Rapped in Romance." We had plenty of fans and we were doing our thing. Shakespeare was the only guy that whenever there was a physical problem on the road, he stood beside me to make sure somebody had my back.

What I didn't know when Cli-N-Tel stayed with Shirley was that he got the same two guys that I got to stand in for Dre and Yella. Shirley booked *them* as the Wreckin' Cru. We're in Texas; they're in Louisiana. Two radio stations are promoting the Wreckin' Cru the same night. Radio stations down south overlap. Small markets—you're in one town and you're in the same station in two or three different towns. Now, the promoter from the fake Cru sends his daughter to our show to see which Cru he has, the real Cru or the fake Cru? We get on stage, she looks at us, and we got the album cover in our hands: that's me, that's Dre, that's Yella.

"No it ain't! I'ma tell my daddy y'all are fake, we got the real Cru."

"How you gonna do that? We're right here, okay?"

Needless to say, the promoter they were working with was a shyster sonofabitch from Louisiana. Eventually, not only did he not pay them, but he broke into their hotel room and stole all their shit. So that whole back-stabbing situation

240

was quickly dissolved. But it was crazy because for about two weeks, there were two Wreckin' Cru's, because Cli-N-Tel had put his own Cru together to go on tour and try to offset what we did.

While on tour, we were playing small venues, skating rinks, whatever the case may be. I'll never forget one of the shows we did in Texas at a skating rink. Nobody showed up, and the promoter was playing with our money.

When it comes to my money, I don't play. That's why I don't play with anybody else's money. Don't play with mine, I won't play with yours. I'm old school. So the guy told us to play, but he only had half our money. So we started playing and he told my road manager he would have the rest of the money.

"Start the show; I'll have the rest of the money in a couple minutes."

The manager gave me the green light to start the show. So we're doing the show and we had done about three or four songs when I looked over at my road manager, and he shook his head. That means we still don't have the money. I know from DJ'ing experience that once the show is over, you have no bargaining chips. No power. No power, no pay.

As I've done in the past with party promoters, I immediately had a technical problem that could only be resolved with immediate payment. I stopped the show, and I'm having Yella play trying to figure out what's going on. I knew what was wrong—I had turned the switch off.

So the promoter walks over and gives the road manager the rest of the money and kicked over my rack of keyboards. Now I'm fixin' to whip his ass. I go after him. There was a security guard standing by him. I ran past Dre and Yella, grabbed the security guard's flashlight, took it out of his little holster, and was going to clobber this cat because he had kicked over about five grand worth of equipment. The only person that stood with me in defending what was ours (or really, mine) was Shakespeare, but he was trying to talk sense to me.

> "Man, don't whip his ass right now; too many witnesses, and you don't wanna go to jail in Texas!"

I thank Shakespeare right now for not letting me whip that guy's ass.

41

Swamp Dog

While on tour, we swing home to play the Long Beach Arena with the Force M.D.s, Sir Mixalot and the Rappin' Duke. I meet a young lady backstage and we start talking. Shortly after, she takes me home to meet her parents. This is when the music game changed for me.

Michelle's mom and dad are in the record business. Her dad is Jerry Williams, a blues singer known as Swamp Dog. He was a short, squeaky-voiced guy, one of the funniest men I ever met. Nice guy. Reminded me of Joe Tex. Her mom, Yvonne, was a tall, good-looking woman in great shape for her age. She had a personality that gave her the versatility to be a nun or a prison guard. She was one of the sweetest women I ever met, but she "didn't take no shit." She reminded me a lot of my mom. She and her husband were the ultimate partnership when it came to the record business. He performed, and she managed and promoted him. I thought that was the bomb then, and I still do.

The house was a museum of record memorabilia—laminated Billboard charts on the wall, a huge white grand piano, and this old school juke box up against the wall filled with 45's that he and his fellow recording buddies made over the years. Michelle introduces me.

"Hey dad, listen, this is my friend Lonzo. I met him at the concert. He has a group called the World Class Wreckin' Cru. He got his own label…"

"Oh, yeah? Boy, have a seat!"

He's feeling me out.

"You independent?"

"I think so."

"Are you BMI or ASCAP?"

"I'm BMI."

"You gettin' your royalties quarterly or monthly?"

"What's royalties?"

"Chelle! This dude's too goddamn dumb to go with you! Get this muthafucka out of my house! You got a record label and don't know what royalties are? How you gettin' paid?"

I'm stuttering now.

"We just sell records. I sell some and…"

"Who's your distributor?"

"Macola Records."

"That's the sonofabitch on Santa Monica Blvd., ain't it?"

"Yeah."

"Well shit, how many records you sold?"

"I don't know, about twenty-five, thirty thousand."

"Shit—how much money you got?"

"I don't know, he just gave us $25,000 a few weeks ago for our album."

"Man, you crazy! You dumb sonofabitch, you got money you ain't…Chelle, this dude's too dumb to go with you!"

He's clowning me now. I'm feeling about two inches tall. He ain't through with me…

"Come on in the back. Let me talk to you a minute."

We got to talking. He's trying to figure out what I know. I'm supposed to be going to meet the parents and leave. ***Shit.*** Her father took me in the back room and gave me a third-degree mafia-style meeting. I can point to how every time I made a business transition, there was always an older cat putting me up on game. Jefty would put me up on club game. Swamp Dog put me up on music game. Good Fred put us up on distribution. Good Fred distributed all hair care products, but widgets are widgets, okay? Distribution is distribution...

Old School Generals Guiding the Young Soldiers
"I can give you the game, but you don't have to listen"

"Damn, you don't know *nothin'*, do you?"

"Mr. Dog..." (I call him Mr. Dog right to this day.) "I stumbled into this thing, we had a good idea, we have some product, I sold records on the phone…"

He jumps in.

"But man, understand this. You gettin' calls, you on tour, you had to sell records in those territories to go on tour. If you go on tour, if you sell records in that territory, where is the accounting for the records that were sold in the territory?"

These are things I hadn't even thought about! I'm so happy to be on tour, I'm just glad to be on stage doing my thing. I'm like most kids today—I'm doing something I never did before and people are liking me for it. I ain't thought about the business end at all. And I'm supposed to be the boss.

I'm still working with Shirley, but Shirley isn't giving me any information whatsoever. Swamp Dog took me under his wing and made me his project. And I'm crazy 'bout his daughter at the time. In fact, the daughter became upset with me because sometimes we'd have a date and it would turn into we got to go out tomorrow cause pops has got so much game tonight, he's on fire. I'm getting private lectures from an experienced record vet, things I need to know *today*.   This isn't an I-can-use-it-down-the-road opportunity…this is something I can apply tomorrow!

Sure enough, Swamp Dog sits down with me, goes to Macola, and gets us another $25,000! He takes a little piece—I ain't mad at him. Now, his next question…

"Where is y'all giggin' at?"

I told him we had a couple of shows.

"Well shit… if you got a record company, you need somebody working the radio, you need somebody on the road with you—a road manager, you need somebody back at home working your shows."

So he hooked me up with a cat named Randy Ran. Randy Ran was our road manager. We got another guy named John Brown who did phone sales and tracking for us. And Swamp Dog was coordinating our tour. Now the problem I got is, big Shirley has a crush on me, but she's got Dre, Yella and Cli-N-Tel's ear. Whatever she's telling them is totally contradicting what I'm doing with Swamp Dog. They don't know Swamp Dog yet. They think I'm only going for Swamp Dog because I'm sleeping with his daughter. They're not privy to the meetings.

I'm doing these meetings on the weekends and in between rehearsals, whatever the case may be. They're out doing their thing. They think I'm out having fun; I'm actually learning the record business, another angle of it.

Swamp Dog is teaching me the independent game. He's teaching me the value of records. Back then, a record cost me seventy-five cents to make. A box of 50 twelve-inches cost me $37.50, but it's worth $112.50 ($2.25 apiece), $125 if it's a hot record ($2.50 apiece). If I take two boxes to a record store, I could sell them for $112.50, or I could just cash them in for only $100 and let somebody make a profit on the balance.

So now, I've learned all this information. While we're on the road, even when we run out of money, Swamp Dog would send us some records to take to the distributor to pay for our hotel. Or maybe we had to stay overnight, so if we had four or five rooms, as opposed to me paying for it with my cash, Swamp Dog would send the alternative.

> "Hey man, I'ma send you some records. Take 'em to the distributor, cash 'em in, and then take care of your rooms and your food and whatever else you need, 'til the next gig shows up."

This practice is done by all record companies. It's called "free goods." With free goods, you give your records away for promotion, but the artists don't get paid a royalty. This was done to pay for promotional cost for a project. Sometimes the records were given away for free, but most of the time they were sold to stores at a discounted rate to assist with the financing of the promotion of a record. We were doing the same thing in our own way—using the records to pay for our rooms, and no royalties were due.

I told Swamp Dog about Shirley, how she's supposed to have helped her dad get all this money that was owed to him. Swamp Dog had me ask her this, ask her this, ask her that…

"If she don't tell you this right here, she don't know what she's talkin' about."

So I asked her, and sure enough, she gave me the wrong answers. So I'm suspicious about her so-called experience. Meanwhile, I mentioned to Swamp Dog about the Ebony and Jet thing.

"Muthafucka, you gave her *how much money?*

"$4,000 for an ad in Ebony and Jet."

"Muthafucka, that shit costs about $20,000 per magazine, and you gave her $4,000? Oh, you got to be a **god**damn fool!"

He looked at me like I was out of my goddamn mind.

"Muthafucka, you can't buy a staple for $4,000 at Ebony or Jet magazine! How the hell is she gonna buy

two ads? Man, leave that bitch alone and let me put together you a team so you can go make yourself some goddamn money! You with my daughter...you just can't be doing no dumb shit! You's about a dumb sonofabitch, huh?"

So now I'm ready to cut Shirley loose, but because of that little orgy in the back of the bus on the way home from the Pittsburgh (California) gig, my Cru was saying no. Now I'm on the outside. I see what's happening. I got played; worse, *we* got played. I'm trying to save us, but she has screwed her way into their heads, literally, and there's nothing I can say.

While I was trying to find a way to keep everybody happy and keep Shirley on the team, I was leaning more toward Swamp Dog since he knew what he was doing. Swamp Dog taught me the music game as an independent label owner—he taught me how to make money, how to stay paid.

"Look man," he told me, "before you started fuckin' with my daughter, you didn't know who I was, did you?"

"No."

"I do very few gigs this side of the Mason-Dixon line. I sell about twenty thousand CD's a year. I might make $200,000. I do a gig, I get three or four thousand a night. If I do about twenty gigs a year, I can make another sixty grand a year. I'm supposed to be a Swamp Dog, and nobody don't even know me! I found a niche! It's a lot of money sittin' between where I am and where Michael Jackson is, or whoever else is supposed to be on top. Bottom line is, if this is what you love, you ain't got to sell your soul to do what you love. Find you a niche and you just wear it out 'til it don't work no more!"

That goes back to the same thing I said earlier: *"Do what you love, you'll never work hard a day in your life."* Add to that, *"find what people need, they'll always need you"* and *"find a niche and wear it out 'til it don't work no more"*...these are three things that I live by. Living by these simple rules has allowed me to be self-employed for nearly forty years, and all doing what I love—entertainment.

42

Real Eyes Realize Real Lies

Not long after I graduated high school, Ronald Reagan terminated the CETA program. When young, energetic minds and bodies have nothing positive to focus that energy on, it can be a recipe for disaster. With no teen community activities, no movie theaters or skating rinks in the area—they're gonna follow whatever example there is to follow, no matter what it is.

Kids don't think. I remember as a teen going to see karate movies and watching the actors kick ass and break boards with their heads and hands on screen. And guess what my dumb-ass friends and I did? We immediately went to my house, went behind my garage and grabbed some wood—a 2x4 and some plywood. Then we went in the garage and we tried our best to break the boards with our hands and foreheads. I fractured my hand and I had a big-ass knot on my head (and a big-ass scab later).

Face it—kids are stupid! We all did stupid shit as kids. The difference is that we weren't constantly bombarded with negative images. And we had our elders, who we dared not disrespect, to put us back on track at any given moment. So as modern-day artists compete for attention by saying and doing most anything to get more "likes" or hits on social media, it's all done at the cost of our kids' future.

Kids today are not allowed to make kid-mistakes without having adult consequences. As a stupid young man at Van Guard Junior High in Compton, I was notorious for popping girls' bra straps. Back then, the girl would chase me, she might hit me back or we'd wrestle…it was teenage foreplay. The most that would happen was I'd get called to the vice principal's office. I might have gotten a swat if the girl made a big deal of it or didn't like me.

Nowadays, that same stupid act will not only get you a sexual assault case and a court date, it's the first step into the "Prison Industrial Complex."

The crazy part is, when I was a kid, when you turned eighteen your record was erased and you got a fresh start on life and the law. Now, *anything* you do as a minor can follow you into adulthood magnifying your sentence for whatever you are currently accused of. This can land you in a cell for a long time.

Not only are kids being desensitized to crime, but also to basic responsibility with lyrics like *"I knew my rent was gonna be late a week ago, but I gotta party tonight."* This subliminal messaging doesn't only benefit the prison industrial complex, but also the other hood vultures like the payday loan industry.

It's hard to get jobs with bad credit or a bad driving record. *"Rolling down the street smoking Indo sipping on gin and juice"* is a 502 DUI if you get caught. You can't get a job driving for Uber with a DUI. Bottom line—youngsters make bad decisions they have to pay for, either with time or money.

Back in the day when I was a kid, my dad questioned me when I had money. I couldn't bring dirty money into his house! If my mom had been alive, she'd have done the same thing. But at some point in time, some parents stopped questioning where kids got the money from; they just paid some bills and momma prayed, *God don't let him get shot, don't let him go to jail—God, look out for him!*

In the beginning the subject matter was so derogatory, you had people like C. Delores Tucker who campaigned against it for a while. But after a while it started making so much money that most of the community turned a blind eye and accepted it. The integrity of the Black community was bought and sold for money and hoping for a way out.

Askia...

"We have to look at society and ask ourselves why the African American community stood by and

allowed this type of thing to be developed in their own community. The whole community has a responsibility.

"Our parents listened to a different type of music than we did. Now you have a 39 year old grandma—she's just as much into gangsta rap as a 15 year old kid."

Meanwhile, laws are changing for programs like Section 8. You cannot house a felon if you're housed under the Section 8 program, making it harder for men out of prison to find places to stay, even with family members or a girlfriend. So now, being stuck between a rock and a hard place with limited options, some feel they have to do what they have to do to survive. This could mean going back to the same thing that got them locked up in the first place.

We are the only race in the world that has rewarded artists for literally promoting genocide. That's part of why I'm doing this book. ***We're the only people in the world that support entertainers who promote genocide.***

I got a story about a guy from Compton, true story. He came to my studio to record a song, and he's there rapping. Now I've been knowing this young guy since he was about fifteen or sixteen years old. He was about twenty-four or twenty-five at that time. He used to come to Eve After Dark. He's rapping about how "in the Pen we do this, in the Pen we do that…," glorifying going to the penitentiary. I had to ask him…

"When did you go to the Pen?"

He answered, and I quote, "I ain't been to the Pen *yet*."

"Huh?"

"I ain't been to the Pen yet. I did a little County time. I went to Wayside. I ain't been to the Pen yet."

That's what he told me! So time passes by. His partner that was with him that day in the studio, I saw him somewhere years later.

"Hey doc, what's up with you?"

"How you been?" he answers.

"Man, where your boy at?"

"*Fuck* that nigga!"

"Why?"

"Man, that muthafucka got to lying to the Feds about how he was running shit in Compton. He got twenty-five years to life; got me ten years for being in the car with the muthafucka…"

He had talked himself up on twenty-five years, and his boy got ten years just for being in association! *Fed* time, which means you gotta do eighty-five percent! Artists have made it so palatable and so acceptable to do and say certain shit 'til the city almost *had* to live up to what they were talking about!

Yeah, there was a lot going on in Compton. You had all kinda things going on, and by it being a Black city, the media magnified it even more. What people don't understand is the same thing happens in almost every small city around Los Angeles. The difference is, when things happen in other small cities, it tends to get suppressed by the media. When it happens in Compton, it gets *magnified*. Other cities have been able to protect their brand. Compton's brand has never been protected. A friend of mine in law enforcement told me the same shit happens in other communities, but you don't hear it being glamorized in songs and turned into hip hop fairy tales.

Everybody knows that the mafia exists, but the last thing any of *them* (mafia) would ever tell you is that there is a mafia!

"Mafia? Ain't no mafia!"

But every artist with lips is rapping about being a gangsta, being a mafia, being on somebody's gang. Then you got kids seeing this shit, growing up on this shit, and then it perpetuates a lot of the negativity that only feeds the prison industrial complex. Worse of all, it makes it seem cool—and kids love cool. I know I did.

The CDC and other private prison corporations reap huge profits, benefiting off the demise of Black and Latino youth that are desensitized to killing and committing crime. Meanwhile, black and brown brothas' lives are being traded on the stock exchange like pork bellies and soy beans.

43

America Loves a Gangster
Don't try this at home

Once upon a time, I was one of those young, impressionable, stupid-ass kids. I wanted to be a Black Panther, but I couldn't—I was a Catholic School kid and momma wasn't having that.

Because it was the flavor of the day, I *did* have a natural. I wore an army coat with the peace symbols on it. I walked around going, *"Peace."* I did that; I did what was kosher for that time.

When Super Fly came out and it became cool to have the perm, I was one of the first guys to get my hair fried! I'm

one of the first guys who went to school with ears blistered because I was trying to get my hair pressed! When I got to school with my press and curl on, guys called me gay; called me a faggot. But the very guys that called me a faggot got their hair pressed two days later, and *still* wear a perm today in what's left of their hair!!

At sixteen, I was impressed by the Superfly album poster. Yes, the *poster*, not the movie. I couldn't go see the movie; I just saw the album poster. I know what it did to me as a kid to see this cool guy, maxi coat, the fly hair style.

On the back of the album cover it showed he was a cocaine dealer. I found out what cocaine looked like and I found me a stash of some baking powder, and man, I was sniffing that shit trying to play like I knew what I was doing! I didn't do it around dudes who knew what cocaine was, but the dudes who didn't know thought I was a cool muthafucka! All because of what I saw on the album cover!

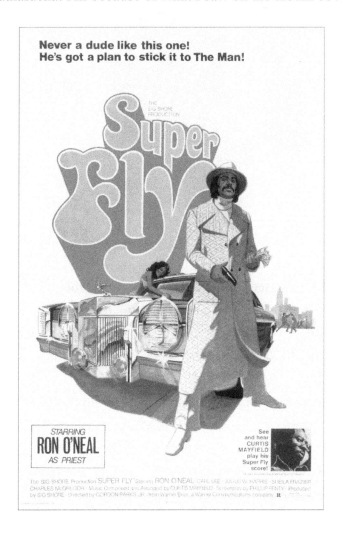

Yes, I was sixteen years old…yes, I was stupid…but guess what! If they had told me at that time that shooting niggas was something to do, I might'a done that too, because in my mind, I didn't know any better! I was gullible!

I **know** how influencing this music is! **I** did this dumb shit! What people don't realize is that the same producer that produced a lot of the positive Black Power music of that time, Curtis Mayfield, also did Super Fly. Curtis Mayfield had songs like People Get Ready…these are theme songs that I grew up on in the late 60's, early 70's.

All of a sudden, Curtis Mayfield stops singing about Black unity; he's singing about Super Fly! He had that much power and influence to change the direction of the streets! Same thing with gangsta rap! The gangs were in the streets. Gangs became more powerful in the early 70's. They were always around, but the numbers were nowhere near as large as they became in the 80's and 90's. The Crips were formed in the early 70's—you *had* to be a gang banger because you were from the hood. Back then, they went on *quality* of guys, not quantity. Guns were limited, but it was all about fighting—"thumping." If a guy could thump, they wanted you on the team, they wanted you in the gang.

I lived in a different neighborhood. I lived in a Blood neighborhood. I couldn't be in my neighborhood gang; I was too skinny. *But!* I had protection because I had a car, and I would take them to dances with me. I'd drop them off to do some of their dirt; sometimes I'd put nine guys in the station wagon, drop 'em off, and they'd get rid of me quick.

"Get the fuck outa here! *Now!*"

I clearly remember taking some of those same guys home in my dad's lawnmower truck after a house party—a truck filled with lawnmowers!—and I got the neighborhood thugs stacked up on the back as we rolled down Rosecrans headed to the house. As far as they were concerned at that time, my dad's lawnmower truck might as well have been a limousine.

Even when they'd be getting high or smoking cigarettes, they wouldn't let me be around them. Some of these guys were a couple of years older, some were my age, some were even younger, but they knew I was on a different path. Plus my dad and mom would have had a FIT if they caught them guys giving me a joint or a cigarette. They knew, *hey, get this kid away from 'round here…we don't want him to be nowhere around our shit when it's going down. Plus he's a square. He ain't for this.*

That was the difference between when I grew up and what happened in the late 80's and early 90's. I think what happened is because gangsta rap was the first musical genre to give theme music to the street dealer. Up until then, it was all anti-gang, *don't* do drugs, *don't* do this right here.

People were recording songs like "We're All in the Same Gang" and "Self-Destruction." But for the most part, you just had a handful of gangsters. Boogie Down Productions, Poor Righteous Teachers and Public Enemy were all focused on political issues and raising the consciousness level of the youth.

On one of N.W.A.'s first albums, Dre's line was "I don't smoke weed or stress, because it makes you another sequel, makes you and a sucker equal." The next big album he did was The Chronic! It was so dope that it seemed to bring a new awareness to smoking weed. It became fashionable to have a blunt hanging out your mouth. It was like the world had made a new discovery of shit we had done for decades.

The media focuses on what makes more money, so if selling out a generation of people to make a dollar will increase the stocks of a particular corporation while raising the visibility of certain artists, as long as it's gonna make them money, off to jail you go! Might as well call it what it is: ***21st century slave labor in the prison industrial complex***.

On the same token, if the same corporation could make a profit elevating the mindset of the same generation of folks, we would all be college scholars. All they want to do is make money. Until more people understand that, we will all be lost. The game is chess, not checkers, although the boards look just alike. It goes back to one of my life-lessons, *"give people what they want and they will always want you."*

Part VII

Responsibility

"To Whom Much is Given..."

44

All Eyes on Us

I'm glad I waited to see the movie Straight Outta Compton before completing this book. First of all, I want to give Kendrick Lamar a personal shout-out for looking out for Centennial, my alma mater, and the City of Compton the way he has. Also, I'm proud that Dre has stepped up and decided to donate his funds from the "Compton" album to build a Performing Arts Center in Compton. Hopefully it will give somebody else in our hometown or the surrounding area the opportunity to do something historical following in the footsteps of the pioneers and the legends from Compton.

I can take pride in my role as a hip hop pioneer, but I have concerns about the collateral damage resulting from fans being unable to separate some of the artists from the characters they portrayed. Still, I never stop watching. It's like you have kids that don't really come around much, but you still keep an eye on them from a distance.

In the game of life, people get famous. Being a role model is a byproduct of being famous. When Charles Barkley said, "I ain't nobody's role model," my reaction was *that's not true! Yes you are!* When you step your ass out on stage, or on that basketball court, or that football field, or that baseball diamond, you automatically inherit the opportunity, and the *power* to influence somebody else. In fact, when you walk into your own business or people see your nice house or pretty wife, or you roll down the street in your nice car, kids want to know what road you took to achieve these things.

For example, one of my local role models was Lonnie Simmons of Total Experience Records. I would go to his club, the Total Experience on Crenshaw, to see him get out of his Rolls Royce well-dressed and walk into his club, and listen to the DJ play his artist's records in the club (the Gap Band). That impressed me so much as a young man, guess what I did! Became a club owner, label owner, and love being clean. I never in my life spoke to Lonnie, I never shook the man's hand. I just saw him and he impressed me.

Imagine that impression being magnified by television media compounded over a period of time! We all might own clubs because everyone already has a record label. Being a role model is a byproduct of being a person of focus.

Just like smoke is a byproduct of fire, being a role model is a byproduct of fame. Everybody wants to know how you got there. They watch how you play the game; they watch how you live your life. If it worked for you, maybe it will work for them.

Cats walk up to me and tell me how I've influenced them.

> "Man, I wanna be just like you. Man, you do this, you do that, you stay cool, you're the same cat all the time…"

It makes me feel good that people realize that whether I got a million dollars or I'm on my last twenty, I'm the same guy.

45

Summing It Up

In west coast hip hop's infancy, I was the leader. I am a leader. Unfortunately, I cannot control what others say about me. I have literally watched my role in hip hop be reduced from being a pioneer to being just a friend of Dre's, along with a variety of demeaning comments.

It's important that people understand *my* story. Most people try to start the story of west coast hip hop with N.W.A., overlooking the fact that N.W.A. was spawned from Lonzo and Kru-Cut Records. My story has been minimized, misconstrued, misquoted—all kinda shit. My name is not easily recognized unless you're a hip hop enthusiast. If you're a hip hop enthusiast, then you know about Lonzo.

It's important that my story gets told properly. I'm not a great rapper; I'm not a great producer. I'm just a great opportunist. I've had the opportunity to be a part of Dre's career, of Ice Cube's career, of Eazy E's career.

Not many in the industry, especially hip hop, can say all that came from one person. The roots in my flow chart run deep. When you look at west coast hip hop and rap, I had a hand in most of what took place.

I was a DJ (still am), but because of my entrepreneurial training and leadership, I could open the door for guys that couldn't open the door for themselves. They didn't have the kind of initiative or foresight to try to do these things. They didn't have that kind of entrepreneurial spirit.

I learned a lot back in the day creating and growing with the World Class Wreckin' Cru. Looking back, some things started making sense. Watching the movie called "Chess Records" immediately made me think of my record company, Kru-Cut Records. It was the hub of so many careers that exist today. Kru-Cut Records and my studio launched Dr. Dre, Ice Cube, and Eazy E. There were also Michel'le, MC Eiht, and PG-13—some of these guys you might not really know.

When you do the lineage of all the acts that came from Dre, Cube, and Eazy, they were part of my hub that's *full* of spokes—Dre got Snoop Dogg, Warren G, Nate Dog, and the Dogg Pound, Eminem, and Fifty Cent and his crew. Cube has the West Side Connection, Mack 10 and

272

everybody that Mack 10 collaborates with. So when you take a look at the hub of West Coast Hip-Hop, there is no stronger hub than Kru-Cut Records.

And when you look at how much money has stemmed from the hub of Kru-Cut Records, this hub has produced grandchildren, with me being the creator—the father of Kru-Cut Records, which is the middle, the foundation. DJ Unknown and Ice T are offspring. DJ Unknown owned Techno Hop Records, which produced Ice T and King T. Later, Unknown picked up DJ Slip, MC Eiht, and Compton's Most Wanted.

My point is, looking at this hub confirms one thing: my hub has produced a billion dollars' worth of people that stemmed from Kru-Cut. That's all that I'm saying. Kru-Cut was that one common denominator, and it inadvertently made history. Don't get me wrong, Macola had some, but not every artist came from them; in fact, Macola got business through Kru-Cut.

I'm just one person. I do what I can to give the community options other than crime or prison…

Askia…

"Right now, Lonzo's running pretty much the only club in the community! In West L.A., I can find bars and clubs everywhere—young ones have a way to release

the tension they built up during the week. "Lonzo has a strong positive influence to this day—even more so now. At this point in time he brings something greater back to the community. When he was young, he was trying to do something for the money. Now he's trying to do something to really assist.

"Back in the day, his counterparts were maybe six years younger than him. Now they're twenty-six years younger than him. That's a whole different scenario, but he's bringing that wisdom and knowledge and understanding."

I don't really have any regrets—if I did have one, I guess it would be that I didn't have Dre under a longer contract! But I ain't mad at nobody. I just want people to understand that no matter what we try to do, especially when you're the first one doing it, you are inadvertently making history.

And as Black folks, our history is already distorted with omissions and lies. So while I'm still here, I'm telling mine—first hand, straight from the horse's mouth. Another West Coast first.

When you are really pioneering, with no roadmap to follow, you make mistakes and you just have to learn as you go along. And you **better** have thick skin, or you won't last. You might not have any shady motivation whatsoever, but mistakes will take on legendary proportions, even when the complainers helped you make them, until they practically overshadow the great things you've done for yourself *and* your team. Thick skin is key, and a slow temper. You don't disprove lies by blowing up about it.

This story needed to be told right—I hate seeing history fucked up, especially when it is mine. I refuse to argue with another publicist about shit I did—or did not do. It's more important for me at this point in my life for the truth to be acknowledged than it is for me to be a hero.

I gotta close reiterating that I am not a hater; I'm an educator and a creator. Since I'm not a multi-millionaire, my story may not be seen to hold a lot of validity by those who only use dollars to keep score. But understand this, it's the most truthful story that you're going to get.

I am really proud of Dre's and Cube's success. I could not be more proud if they were my own sons. Their success has given and will continue to give me a legendary foothold on west coast hip hop.

Whether you call it hip hop, rap, or gangsta rap, it still has a lot of power to influence lives. I know two or three people can't change the whole world by themselves, but a genre sure can change a mental attitude. It did it once; *it can do it again.*

What more can I say? It is what it is.

Kru-Cut's Deep Roots

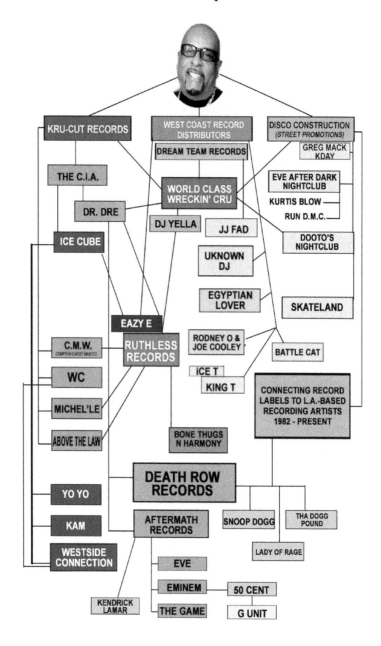

About The Author

Alonzo "Lonzo" Williams is the only entertainer and club owner from his era still DJ'ing and providing club entertainment to his community. He's the first of his peers from back in the day to write a book documenting the early rise of west coast hip hop. He hosts a live weekly Blog Talk Radio program called "Live With Lonzo" on the High Frequency Network, 12:00 noon to 12:45 p.m. He lives in Los Angeles near Compton, California, and is very active in the community.

Contact Lonzo:
Email Lonzo@lonzowilliams.com
Facebook: Alonzo Lonzo Williams
Twitter: RealLonzoNWA
Instagram: RealLonzoNWA
YouTube: Lonzo Williams

CPSIA information can be obtained
at www.ICGtesting.com
Printed in the USA
BVHW041713190322
631937BV00007B/39